WANDERING WHEELS

WANDERING WHEELS

JACK HOUSTON

BAKER BOOK HOUSE
Grand Rapids, Michigan

1

"Where ya headed?"

It's July, 1966. McConnellsburg, Pennsylvania. A dozen bicycle riders roll into a Gulf service station along U.S. Highway 30 and dismount. All the young men are teen-agers, with the exception of one man in his thirties, who apparently is their leader.

The riders, their skin tanned and their hair bleached, glisten in the afternoon sun, their bodies beaded with perspiration. The group quickly forms two lines — one at the cold drink machine, the other at the rest room. Each young man patiently waits his turn, shoving only in jest.

Mingled with their sounds is the occasional *bong* of the gas station's bell and the sharp laughter from a small group of truck drivers who also have stopped for refreshment. On the road, cars and trucks groan past and gear down to head up the Tuscarora Range of the Allegheny Mountains, their tires ripping off the flypaper pavement.

The odor of warm road tar, grease and oil hang about, pushed aside occasionally by a puff of breeze. Spilled gasoline evaporates from the station's pump apron.

Curious about the group of cyclists, the station attendant, a short, heavyset, elderly man, and the truck drivers move toward the riders congregated at the pop machine. "Where ya headed?" one of them asks. "To Washington, D.C.," he's told.

When asked where they are from, the young men answer, "Taylor University in Upland, Indiana." There are thirty-five of them

7

in all, the curious are told, the others having stopped elsewhere to rest. Their leader is Bob Davenport, head football coach at the small college.

"You're not planning to ride up those mountains?" the station attendant half-asks, half-states to Davenport. He motions to the mountain range before them.

"We sure are," Davenport answers confidently. "How high is it? how much of a grade?"

"It's about twenty-five hundred feet, I'd guess, and about a 15 percent grade. You'll never make it." The attendant looks at the truck drivers, who nod assuringly.

The Tuscarora Range had been threatening the cyclists through the people the riders had met all through Pennsylvania. "Oh, you're riding bikes to Washington?" they'd say. "Wait until you get to the Tuscarora. You'll walk your bikes then."

The riders had half-dreaded meeting up with the range after hearing how tough it was going to be. Now, as the station attendant and the truck drivers laugh and joke together, putting down the riders by telling them they'll never make it to the top, Davenport feels cocky enough to take on a challenge.

"Mister," he says to the attendant, punctuating every consonant, "I'll bet you a buck a head that every one of these kids will make it up the side of that mountain — that without getting off their bikes, they'll ride all the way to the top."

For a moment everyone stands silently. The young men appear excited that their coach has called this man's bluff.

Feeling he's been put in his place, the man says, "A buck a head. . . . Okay, it's a bet!"

"Okay," Davenport confirms. "Every kid that makes it up there without getting off his bike, you pay us a buck; and every kid who doesn't make it without getting off his bike, we'll pay you a buck."

Now the station attendant grows more serious about his questioning of the group. Until this point, he and the others gathered around have assumed that the riders began their trip in Indiana, back at Taylor University. But now the station attendant asks the one significant question he hadn't asked before: "By the way, where did you guys start your trip?"

Davenport tells him: "We started in San Francisco five weeks

"Too bad we didn't get that bet . . . ."

ago, and these fellas have ridden over three thousand miles at this point."

The man's Adam's apple just about bulges out of his throat, and he says, "Well, now, let me reconsider for a moment. . . ." A few minutes later he calls off the bet.

Not long after, the riders — all thirty-five of them — regroup at the bottom of the mountain and begin pedaling up the highway. Within minutes, many of the riders find themselves zigzagging up the grade to cut down the percentage. About an hour later they reach the summit — not one of them having had to get off his bike during the climb. At the top, they pause to rest, many of them thinking, "Too bad we didn't get that bet," reasoning they would have had a great meal off the thirty-five dollars they would have rightly earned.

Even so, the riders are glad they left at the service station below them some of the things they had learned from the experience and adventure of riding a bicycle across America. Many had told how the tour had served as a rugged challenge to each of them, how

9

it had tested how much a man each rider really was, how each had his personal set of values tested in the tough discipline of physical exhaustion and self-reliance.

Others told how they had gained a more realistic picture of their Creator — how He related to their lives as they battled the elements and found themselves utterly dependent upon Him as members of the Wandering Wheels.

Four years later, by the end of the sixties, this organized group of young bike riders — the Wandering Wheels — had crisscrossed the United States more than a half-dozen times: from San Francisco, California, to Rehoboth Beach, Delaware, twice; from San Diego, California, to Savannah, Georgia, once; from Long Beach, California, to Rehoboth Beach, once; from San Francisco to New York City, once; from Miami, Florida, to Seattle, Washington, twice and from Seattle to Washington, D.C., once. More than 350 alumni of the Wandering Wheels had rolled over a total of thirty thousand miles of American highways by the end of the summer of 1970, some riders making more than one of the trips.

Each year in the seventies the Wandering Wheels will log thousands of additional miles as members of this unusual team spend their summer, Thanksgiving, Christmas, and Easter vacations pedaling in parts of America.

Volumes have been written about the American teen-ager — his softness, his conduct, his sophistication, and his boredom. Assessing these conditions of American youth during the early 1960's, Bob Davenport discovered what he calls "an adventure gap." A part of life was not being filled by watching super-heroes on television or by engaging in a number of activities typical of today's youth. Acting on the conviction that he could do something about the adventure gap, Davenport devised and undertook a plan to give young people the adventure they lacked, and coupled it with spiritual renewal.

The result has been Wandering Wheels. Since 1964, when Davenport led his first bicycle tour down along the Mississippi River in search of this adventure and renewal, he has presented to those with whom the Wandering Wheels have come in contact a group of American young people who have been able to conquer themselves by conquering America on a bike.

In 1968, Julian Gromer, a professional photographer from

Grand Rapids, Michigan, who has produced several travelogue films, traveled with the Wandering Wheels for its fourth cross-country tour. By his own initiative and at his own expense, Gromer filmed, edited, and produced a documentary illustrating all the excitement and beauty of the trip. This book, like the film, attempts to capture the spirit and excitement of the Wandering Wheels program without an attempt to glorify its leaders or its riders.

As you read this book, hopefully you will find the Wandering Wheels to be normal human beings with normal failings. You will meet young people who, despite their religious background and training, have difficulty trusting God for what seems to be the impossible. They are young people who dislike praying in a group, who curse the elements, who weep, who fight, who sometimes wish they were dead — yet who sincerely desire to know their Creator better.

Davenport operates his Wandering Wheels program from Upland, Indiana, on the campus of Taylor University, a small, conservative Protestant undergraduate school. Once, more than a century ago, a Methodist seminary for women, today Taylor is a co-educational institution boasting fourteen hundred students. It is a member of the Hoosier College (athletic) Conference.

Before going to Taylor as its head football coach, Davenport had been a two-time All-American fullback for the UCLA Bruins. He was a member of the National Champion team of 1954. He saw action in two Rose Bowl games and had been voted Most Valuable Player in the Hula Bowl. Following college, he had gone to Canada to play pro ball with the Canadian Football League. In 1958 he went to Taylor.

Davenport retired from coaching to devote full time to his Wandering Wheels program in 1969, but he left behind him an impressive record: his Trojans had won five HCC championships in eleven years and he had been named the conference Coach of the Year three times.

One is surprised to learn that Davenport comes from a broken home; he doesn't seem to be the typical product of such a tragedy. After his mother and father separated when he was fourteen, he moved into a foster home where church attendance was much a part of the routine. As a result, Davenport gained a positive intro-

11

duction to the Christian faith to which he later committed his life.

As a result of his Christian commitment, which for him includes daily prayer, Bible reading, and meditation, Davenport has become a bit of a mystic. This is not to his discredit. Knowing this, however, helps those who meet him to understand why he regards life and its varying experiences the way he does. For example, things just don't "happen" to Davenport; they are all a part of God's plan. Davenport lives his whole life with this viewpoint — as do many of his riders.

With this development of Christian character, Davenport has remained as much a man as he ever was. He has become his own living proof of his popular concept that to be a follower of Jesus Christ, one does not need to give up rugged individualism. Fanned by personal embarrassment over some people's image of Christ — both inside and outside the church — Davenport's concept of a manly Christ has come to glow brightly through the Wandering Wheels program.

The high school and college young people who ride with Davenport also seem to have a quality different from that of most young people one hears about today. They are activists, but they are not reactionary. Though most come from conservative Midwestern homes, they recognize the America of their peers.

They know of America's injustices, but they also recognize its justice. They have questioned and found few answers, but they have not as yet lost faith. They understand the disaffection of many of their peers for the American way of life. They, too, know of the double standards, the system that does not live up to what it professes. They, too, know of the threat of military duty in what many consider an unpopular cause. They, too, contrast one generation's shallow materialistic involvement with life, and its exploitation of natural resources and persons for personal gain with the commitment of another generation at all costs.

They cannot, like some of their peers, pretend that America does not exist. It is the America they have come to know by experience. The America the older generations came to know by experience doesn't ring as clearly since it has been removed from Main Street and placed between the covers of a history book.

But unlike some of their peers today, those who have ridden

with the Wandering Wheels and experienced its benefits have come to accept life "like it is," and in the Spirit of Christ.

The full impact of this viewpoint may not be fully realized or appreciated without one becoming a bit of a mystic himself. But even without this personal viewpoint, the reader will find one point clear: in light of the Wandering Wheels, the traditional view of Christ and His followers as pantywaists is unfounded. Or, to put it conversely: a virile young man can be a Christian and still be a man.

Looking back on the Tuscarora incident, Davenport says: "We had been trying to impress upon these people in the gas station that we were doing what we were doing in order to get to know Jesus Christ better. I'll never forget that station attendant backing down in light of what these kids were doing. I'm sure the next time he hears the term *Christian* he'll remember that these ornery kids with their bikes in hand had put him down, and that he didn't have the guts to go ahead with the bet."

2

"Okay, God. The summer's Yours."

Davenport conceived of his idea for the Wandering Wheels in 1963. A few years before at UCLA, he had gained some strong Christian convictions, mainly under the influence of a man named Bill Bright and his organization, Campus Crusade. Through this influence, Davenport discovered what he describes as "a dynamic, exciting, unapologetic brand of Christianity — a real positiveness associated with the Christian experience."

Much of this experience became part of Davenport in those college years in the fifties, and because of his own Christian example as a star fullback, who later went into pro football, and then into coaching, he found himself being asked continually by well-meaning groups to speak about his faith to young people.

"I guess they were looking for a big, ornery guy who could assure kids that they weren't sissies or that they weren't out to lunch or that they didn't swing if they were Christians."

Admittedly, Davenport was not a preacher. His real strength in speaking was his athletic background. He could get away with saying things to kids that no preacher could. It was easy for him to impress kids.

He gathered a good repertoire of jokes and a small list of points he wanted to put across, and for a number of years he seemed to be able to hold the young peoples' attention. But after several years of this type of ministry, a pattern was developed that was reworked and overworked to the point where Davenport found he was unimpressed with his own potential in reaching young people. He also disliked the environment in which he had to communicate. "Church-type gatherings just didn't seem to be the ideal place to talk about God to young people," he says. "I became frustrated with the traditional way of trying to communicate with kids by stuffing them into a room and putting some bird up front to talk to them for an hour, hoping that something would happen to them."

". . . saying things to kids no preacher could."

He noticed, too, that the kids weren't listening to him as they used to. "I was there; they were there; but their brains were out in the boondocks somewhere."

His discovery was not unique for the sixties, when young people had few heroes and many were even becoming anti-hero in attitude. The idea of a football hero, for many, had been overworked. It turned many of them off. Even so, Davenport wanted to reach young people. "I came to the conclusion," he says, "that I had better get out in the boondocks with them."

Davenport describes his itching desire as "wanting to see kids there on the edge of their seats with their eyelids bugging out, just waiting to grab some significant bit of information." It wasn't happening in the structured setting — the religious youth meetings. As he puts it: "I was wasting my time — and God's time — coming into the situation under someone else's game rules; it just wasn't coming off right."

The moment of change came in the spring of 1963 as Davenport was driving home from such a weekend of speaking engagements. "I was coming home from Springfield, Illinois," he tells. "I was driving back to Upland on a Sunday afternoon. Saturday night I had spoken at a Youth for Christ rally, and then I was asked to stay overnight and speak in a small church the next morning.

16

"The extra speaking engagement would help out with the trip's finances — I did this often, taking it for granted that this is the way the Lord would have it. But to tell you the truth, this kind of arrangement was a little bit of a drag on me, and I felt a little false hanging around for another meeting just for the extra twenty-five dollars in order to make ends meet. I felt I wasn't maximizing my time.

"I spoke in the church the next morning. It was a noisy service, actually the world's worst environment in which to communicate the truth about God. Of course, the people were appreciative that I had come to speak to them, and they showed the usual, kind spirit as they shook my hand at the door.

"I got into my '63 Falcon and began heading back home on the interstate highway, and during that drive I developed in my person a desire to take my life and use it in such a way that God would really be glorified with what I was doing.

"Sure, I could 'wow' some kids, but I wasn't getting through to most of them beyond the fact that I was an athlete. I wanted them to know me as a person — as God's person. I didn't want to be put up on some kind of a pedestal to be gawked at; I wanted to be accepted as one of them. I would rather have spent three minutes running with them than three hours teaching them in some classroom.

"Suddenly, I had the fantastic urge to tell God, with no strings attached, I was going to give my summer to Him. It was my time to give, not having to coach in the summer. I could do anything I wanted with it.

"I wanted to be the right guy in the right place at the right time. I wanted an experience in really communicating to kids what I knew about Jesus Christ.

"As I was sitting there in the driver's seat, it was almost as if God said, 'Okay, Bob, give Me your summer.' At first I hesitated, but then I answered, 'Okay, God. The summer's Yours.' I'll tell you right now, I had a prayer experience right then that I had never had before, and have never had since.

"After it was all over, I stopped the car to call Barb, my wife, to tell her what had happened. I said, 'Honey, I want you to know that your husband has had a fantastic experience in his

17

Christian life, and in case I don't make it home alive, I want you to know that I've had a meeting with God.' "

That summer Davenport had several opportunities offered him. He finally landed on a Bible conference ground that, as far as environment was concerned, really wasn't too impressive. He was asked to head up a program for the working staff at Winona Lake, Indiana, Conference Grounds.

"The kids were usually worked like dogs," Davenport says, "and little thought had been given to planning any program that would develop character traits. I was told to give them a good time, and to help them find a meaningful spiritual experience.

"I knew we could have a ball and still wind up the summer seeing changes in our lives. I just couldn't wait to get hold of these kids and mold them for Jesus Christ."

That summer Davenport led the staff workers into some of the wildest fun of their lives. They built a mud hill and played "King of the Mountain," looking like a bunch of otters sliding down the hill. They fought together in buildings, broke up old, discarded furniture, held scavenger hunts, and at one point shook the community enough to have the cops out looking for them.

"The kids were always excited," Davenport says, assessing the experience. "When it came time to settle down and study the Bible, they were ready. They went at it with real openness, and as a result their lives were changed."

Looking back at that summer after returning to Taylor in the fall, Davenport felt that he had really been in his realm. Yet, as he returned to teaching and coaching, he continued to look for meaningful ways to reach the minds of young people.

It was then that the bicycle came to his mind. About two years before he had toyed with the idea of riding a bicycle solo across the United States. He was closing out his competition years as an athlete (he was thirty at the time) and wanted to do something exciting and adventuresome before he was too old.

There had been a block of time in his life when the bicycle had been particularly significant. It was while he was a boy, growing up in California. During World War II bikes were popular with all boys, but they weren't readily available. Davenport recalls that as a boy many times he walked out of his house at night and looked up at the stars and prayed for two things: the end of the war and a bike. The materials to manufacture bikes were needed for the war effort, and bicycles just weren't available.

When the war finally ended in 1945, young Davenport started attending a boys' club. It met in an old Japanese church in Long Beach. Soon after he began attending, the military gave the club scores of bicycles.

"They weren't whole bikes," Davenport remembers. "They were in bits and pieces. By our work at club we could earn parts of a bike and eventually earn enough parts to put together a whole bike."

At the age of eleven, Davenport had earned the parts he needed to build his own bike. He built a thin-tire variety, not at all popular in the States then. He sanded it down and painted it several times. He tuned it to perfection. It was a beautiful piece of equipment. But as soon as he could, he traded it off for the more popular balloon-tire bike.

He tuned that bike too, and he rode it regularly until he was a junior in high school — something few among today's more sophisticated youth would do.

"I wasn't embarrassed about riding a bike in high school," he says. "I was a regular swinger on campus — athlete, dance club president, a regular social hot dog."

Now as Davenport began thinking again about a solo cycling trip across the U.S., he found himself saying, "Why spend such a great experience only on yourself? Why not take a bunch of kids with you? You could use your enthusiasm for the bike and desire for adventure to complement your teaching."

Still, Davenport recognized that the bicycle carried with it several potential hang-ups for teen-agers. "The bicycle is death to many of them," he explains. "By the time a kid reaches his teens, all he can think of is 'four-on-the-floor,' and nothing else.

"But I felt that if I could get them interested in the adventure associated with cycling — such as pedaling one hundred miles a day — I might be able to reach them."

So, during that school year of 1963-64 Davenport decided he would take one hundred boys across America with him. He soon realized, however, that it would take all the resources he had to take just ten or fifteen guys with him on a thousand-mile trip.

George Smith, a former Taylor athlete, worked with Davenport to help plan the trip. Davenport took some risks with his own money, bought a 1947 flatbed truck, took out a bank loan and, with Smith and some other fellows on the Taylor campus, began to build a back end for the little red truck.

George Smith had graduated from Taylor in June of '63 and was teaching math in nearby Marion, Indiana. He had several characteristics that fit well into the Wandering Wheels program. He was a tough athlete, for one, having competed at Taylor in football, baseball, and handball. According to Davenport, George could walk on his hands as well as he could on his feet, meaning that figuratively as well as literally.

George was also sensitive to the spiritual implications of the Wandering Wheels concept. He, like Davenport, was somewhat of a mystic. He has since gone on into the Methodist ministry.

Another one of his strong points was his ability to play the guitar and to sing folk music. Prior to committing his life to the ministry, George had played and sung in night spots. Now this ability to play the guitar and sing all kinds of music which appealed strongly to the teen-agers proved another one of his strong points in the Wandering Wheels program.

George became Davenport's co-laborer in the Wandering Wheels effort. Together they planned the Wheels' first trip down the Great River Road. Together they organized the Wheels' second trip through the North Central states. And at one point when Davenport was thinking seriously of giving up the whole idea, it was George's encouragement that finally lifted him out of the doldrums and spurred him on.

"There were several times in the middle of all that planning that I felt like backing out," explains Davenport. "I felt we were getting in a little deep. I was going to have entrusted to me fourteen guys whose lives I was going to put out on the highway to fight with traffic and do several other things that would entail great risk."

But with the bikes purchased, the truck bed rebuilt, and with fourteen kids signed up and ready to go, Davenport left Upland with George Smith in the summer of 1964 and his first crew of inexperienced riders.

3

"He went zoo over them."

The important thing to Davenport in launching the Wandering Wheels concept was to break away from a mode of teaching that had not worked for him in recent years.

"The desire had become so real to me and so serious that I was unable to see things happen. As a result of committing myself to God's plans, I found myself coming up with the first expression of teaching the Christian life through some way other than that of the classroom or church service."

The camper built on the back end of the flat-bed truck could carry the sleeping bags, camping and other necessary equipment, and the boys' bikes. Each rider was required to purchase his own bike, which, for maintenance purposes, had been stipulated as the "Louison Bobet Sports."

"They were a good piece of machinery for the thousand-mile trips," Davenport says.

He and George Smith established their riding route in a way that the people back home could easily identify it. The riders would be transported to the Mille Lacs region, about two hundred miles north of Minneapolis, Minnesota, by car and truck, and from there they would ride their bikes down along the Mississippi River on the Great River Road. They would follow that road through the remainder of Minnesota, through Iowa, into Missouri and Illinois, down to where the Ohio River flows into the

Mississippi at Cairo, Illinois. The trip would take approximately three weeks and would run about a thousand miles.

On an early June morning in 1964, a few moms and dads brought their station wagons to Taylor University and loaded them with riders for the initial part of the trip. Davenport, George Smith, and what riders remained piled into the truck loaded down with the bikes, gear, and other equipment.

"The trip up was a good ego-building experience," explains Davenport. "We enjoyed stopping along the way to eat and telling people what we were about to do."

When they arrived at their destination, they were quick to unload, and then, just as quickly, the moms and dads drove away. Davenport describes that moment as "spooky."

"There I was with fourteen young people. I felt a little bit helpless — like jumping into a lake having never swum before. The thing I'd been dreaming and talking about was now here. I had to begin putting all my thoughts and words into action."

Despite this sudden apprehension, Davenport took to the situation like peanut butter to the roof of the mouth. He took on the role of a first sergeant barking out orders. He appeared to be right in the middle of his element, anticipating along with the other riders the first full-day's ride the next day.

They all were rookies. They knew nothing about riding against the wind or into the sun or about roads with no shoulders that funnel you down along with the big semis, keeping you at the brink of disaster all day long.

Besides this lack of knowledge and not being too well in shape physically, the riders lacked stamina as they mounted their bikes the next morning and pushed off into a west wind. "That wind caused each rider to become completely disillusioned with cycling before we hit the first town," Davenport reports. But mom and dad had left the night before, and the riders were left with their bicycles as the only way of getting down the road.

That first morning they found themselves going to a farmer's door to beg for water. "That was a real introduction to what the pioneers must have experienced," Davenport says. "And that experience introduced us to an element in the program which we hadn't anticipated — an appreciation for the hardships of our forebears."

Many of the riders who had been so cocky, began to eat their words. Several got off their bikes and began walking them into the wind. When they saw the water tower in the first town, they thought it was just ahead — but it turned out to be ten miles away.

When the lead riders finally dragged into the first town, other riders were strung out along the highway for at least five miles. Some continued to walk their bikes, their heads hanging low. Others had stopped to rest along the road, their heads in their hands. All were thinking, "This is the dumbest thing I've ever done — and to think I *paid* to do it."

When Davenport reached the town, he wasn't so proud that he didn't lie down in the grass and rest. He drank water, pop, ate ice cream, candy, everything he could get his hands on. So did the others, and some of the fellows threw up. Of course, several of the townspeople wondered who they were and what they were doing. Their enthusiasm for the project rebuilt the riders' egos as they answered their questions.

But there was more of the first day still ahead of them. After food and rest, the riders started out again. The road turned south from there, and the wind let up.

That night the group finally made it to Lindbergh State Park, just a few miles south of Little Falls, Minnesota. There they found a shelter house with cold showers. It had been a long day — about a twelve-hour ride — and it felt good to wash the salt from their bodies. They had a good rest, then a meal, and then walked into town to loosen up their leg muscles.

They now were one day older and a whole lot smarter. As a result, in the days ahead they would be better able to pace themselves. The next day they would be introduced to the pains of hillclimbing and the thrills and dangers of coasting, which would teach them new lessons about the bicycle and about safety habits. Nearly every new experience brought with it new lessons which Davenport and the others had to incorporate into their pattern of living.

On the fourth day out, the Wheels met a fellow who, as Davenport puts it, "went zoo over them." He was thrilled over what they were doing. He was an American adult who had just about given up on American youth but now fell in love with this group.

He owned a little grocery store in town, and when the Wheels were about to pull out of town the next day, he gave them an amazing amount of food.

"Some perishable food, which he was afraid would spoil before he sold it, and he also gave us several boxes of candied peanuts," Davenport says.

"Up till then, we had been rather conservative in dispensing food — perhaps too conservative. The guys were really thrilled over their abundance of food, which they could bite into whenever they wanted. Of course, we thanked the man, but more than that, we thanked God for this man."

The food sustained the group for the remainder of the trip. From then on the riders looked forward to meeting such men God would send their way. Each day brought with it a new confirmation that this experiment was no mistake, but rather a wall-to-wall adventure. Before long the men were looking forward to the next day's ride, the next place they would stay, and the next people they would meet.

The remainder of the trip was not without its hardships and disappointments. The riders were not without depression. Between Minneapolis and Dubuque, Iowa, the weather took a turn for the worse, and so did the riders. Their response to the elements reminded Davenport of the Israelites' trip through the wilderness as recorded in the Bible. He saw in his own group just how easy it is for a group to become disillusioned.

Rain began soaking the riders about ten o'clock one morning and didn't let up for several hours. It was accompanied by low temperatures, and before long the riders' fingers grew numb. In an attempt to keep warm, they put on extra clothing. But it wasn't foul-weather gear, and soon that too was wet and cold.

"They were not a happy bunch," understates their leader.

Later that day they sloshed into a small town and tramped into a supermarket to dry off. The store manager learned what they were doing and called the mayor. The mayor ordered the firehouse to be warmed up to eighty-five degrees for them. When the guys arrived, they were given coffee and cookies and a place to stretch out to rest. They were dry too soon.

The rain had stopped when they stepped outside again. Thanking their hosts, the Wandering Wheels started out once more, high-spirited and full of enthusiasm. Before an hour passed, however, the rain returned, and so did the irritation.

Davenport knew he would have to find a dry and warm place to camp that night. As he pedaled along through the rain himself, he envisioned a shelter under which they could pull the truck, so that it, too, could dry off. They would need a fireplace to cook the food, dry wood to start a fire, and some electricity for light after an anticipated early darkness.

He wasn't praying for such a place, just thinking about it.

The riders came to a turnoff to a roadside park and started heading down it. The road wasn't too encouraging. To get to the park they had to get off their bikes and walk them because the ruts were six to ten inches deep.

"I remember thinking, 'How could anything good be there, if the road leading up to it is so miserable,'" Davenport recalls.

But as the group rounded the last bend, they found a little shed with a covered fireplace. Under the roof was a dry, concrete slab on which the guys could stretch out their sleeping bags, and there was just enough clearance for the truck. From the shed's ceiling a single light bulb was hanging down by a lone wire — and the light worked!

To top off the experience, the Wheels found that someone had stocked the shelter with a cord of dry wood for the fireplace. "I'll tell you," says Davenport. "I'd rather be there, resting on that concrete slab at 8:30 at night, with the rain dripping off the edge of that shelter, with your clothes drying out by a crackling fire, with good food in your stomach, and with a single light bulb hanging down, listening to guys talk and thanking God for a spot such as this — I'd rather be there than standing in any pulpit under a white steeple, surrounded by stained glass windows and red carpeting."

This would not be the Wandering Wheels' last experience in seeing their needs provided providentially.

Of course, with the exceptional came the usual. And with the usual came guys like George Smith. With all his exceptional points, George was still as human as anyone else. And he had one particularly humorous habit.

George often rode behind the pack with the riders who had fallen behind. As a result, he would sometimes be separated from

". . . you'd better double-check the map. . . ."

the front of the group by several miles, running the risk of missing a turn. On one occasion Davenport and his group of lead riders had crossed a bridge across the Mississippi River and had ridden down the east bank for several miles. When George's group failed to show up at an appointed rest stop, Davenport figured what might have happened and notified the state police. The police located George's group on the west side of the river and informed him of his error — and then told him he would have to take his riders the several miles back to the bridge, since there was no other for many miles in the direction he was headed.

It became a standing joke with the group that if you were riding with George Smith, you'd better double check the map to be sure you were headed in the right direction.

As the days passed on this first excursion, Davenport began to feel that he had found the kind of rapport with the guys for which he was looking. He was riding with them every mile. He was cooking with them, sitting up with them until all hours working on a bike in need of repair, working his heart out with them. They seemed to accept him as one of them.

"It was a great feeling to be able to hand these boys back to their moms and dads in Cairo three weeks later," he says. "— all sun-tanned and in top physical condition. It was also satisfying to know that these young guys had changed spiritually, too. It was even more satisfying to realize that these guys had had a great time, and that they could identify that great experience with their Christian faith. This was what I was looking for."

In the context of adventure, the fourteen young men had devel-

"They seemed to accept him as one of them."

oped mentally and emotionally, spiritually, and physically. Their leaders had too. They had spent some time each day studying the Bible. They had shared their faith with people they met along the way, trying to explain how their experiences were deepening and widening their spiritual lives.

Yes, this did seem to be the kind of experience Davenport was seeking. As he puts it, "I was hooked as far as this type of communication was concerned."

4

Once again, because of the responsibility of taking care of a group of young people on the highway, Davenport had some doubts in his mind about the wisdom of trying another trip. He and the riders had encountered so much they hadn't anticipated. He feared what new experiences another trip might bring.

But not long after the fall semester began at Taylor, Davenport forgot the hardships and the brushes with danger, and all that remained was the glory of bicycle touring. The wanderlust began to return to him, and before long he and George were planning a second trip.

Because he talked the entire school year about what had transpired on the first trip, Davenport found he had more riders than he could handle for his 1965 Wandering Wheels trip.

Davenport obtained another truck and equipped it differently, and in June of that year he and George Smith led an excursion of twenty Wandering Wheels through the North Central United States. This time the trip originated from the Taylor campus and terminated at the same point three weeks and some eleven hundred miles later. They had toured Indiana, Michigan, Ohio, Pennsylvania, West Virginia, and Kentucky. In addition to the purchase of the $85 Bobet bike, the trip cost each rider $50.

A major difference about the second tour was that Davenport signed on a songleader. "Our riders weren't musicians," Davenport is quick to clarify. "We really didn't want them to be. But

29

". . . when the guys sang together, they had a good sound."

the first year we found that when the guys sang together, they had a good sound. So on the second trip we took along a guy who could lead the singing. We had George and a couple of other guys who could play the guitar, and we wrote a theme song to the tune of 'Tumblin' Tumbleweed.' We sang in several churches along the way."

To lead the singing, Davenport took along Dale Senseman. Dale was a 1963 Taylor grad pastoring a small church nearby. In addition, he had musical ability. He and his wife are responsible for the words to the Wandering Wheels song.

Davenport also added a cook to the tour, Bob Uhrich.

Friday, June 5, 1965, was an exciting day for the twenty young riders and their four leaders as they loaded the truck and made last-minute checks on their bikes. They were up at sunrise the next morning and off along the Indiana back roads towards the Michigan state line.

Some sixty-eight miles later they rolled into Chain-O-Lakes State Park near Albion, Indiana, to spend their first night. After a refreshing swim in the lake, they set up camp and prepared supper. When the meal was over, instead of rubbing sore muscles or sacking out for the night, they played a rousing game of touch football.

Later they sang to the strumming of guitars in the light of Coleman lanterns.

The Wheels held their first official concert on the first Wednesday. The riders followed a police escort into Plymouth, Ohio, where they were served a huge smorgasbord provided by several of the town's churches. Nearly two hundred people showed up to hear them sing in the local ball park. After the concert the young men shared some of their experiences of the trip.

They were favorably accepted. Immediately following the concert, a bicycle dealer in town rushed up to invite the group to his shop for some homemade ice cream. The Wheels were glad to oblige.

The days ahead were filled with adventure and work, and were not without their difficulties. More than half-way through their trip, as they returned through Ohio, the young men were scheduled to arrive in a small town named Jewett before sundown. However, the ride that day proved to be more difficult than anyone had anticipated.

When the riders failed to show up, someone sent out a pickup truck in search of them. The Wheels were discovered more than fifteen miles from their destination. It was nearly 10:00 P.M. before the riders rolled into town, and those who had been farthest away rode in on the back of the pickup.

The next morning, Sunday, the young men were received enthusiastically in two churches. Following the services, they were invited to some homes for dinner. They showed their deep appreciation by devouring everything in sight.

On June 23 the Wandering Wheels rolled home to Upland, Indiana. As they dismantled the truck rigging, folded their tents, and cleaned up, the young and tough riders seemed strangely silent. Living, pedaling, cooking, camping, studying, and praying together for three weeks, sharing every bit of each other's hardship, had done something to fuse this group together. For another thing, these guys had learned, just as the riders on the first trip had discovered, that God belonged not only in the cathedral on Sunday, but in every experience of life, every day of the week.

5

"He could literally ride circles
around the other riders."

In addition to those already mentioned, there were other persons associated with the Wandering Wheels in its early days who have since become synonymous with the program. A fellow who became part of the Wheels in its formative years is Dale Murphy. Known affectionately by the riders as "the Murf," he and Davenport have been recognized over the years as the two main people behind the Wheels.

Murf knew of the program from the very start. He was a student at Taylor in 1963, and Murf added to the program his own peculiar type of personality. "He was up on everything," explains Davenport. "He was the kind of guy you could ask about anything, and he would answer you like a prof."

The guys could ask him about stocks and bonds, and he'd have all the answers. On the trips he could fill in the riders on every kind of plant species they'd see along the way or every star that would appear in the sky. Ask him about combustion engines and it was the same story. There was little you could talk to him about that he couldn't discuss intelligently.

Dale came into the program as a volunteer helper after his graduation from Taylor in 1966. As they rode from place to place in the years that followed he would gather fragments of history about the places the Wheels stayed and share them with the riders, adding a new dimension to the program.

His job consisted mainly of bird-dogging, making out daily

33

schedules, taking care of the mail, and lining up places to shower and bed down for the night. Murf did his job from the seat of a Honda 90cc motorcycle. And on the first trip the Wandering Wheels made across America, he took along a 16mm movie camera to film the action. He and Davenport used the film to promote the program and to raise funds for new and better equipment.

Murf joined the Wandering Wheels staff in 1969 as a full-time, paid worker.

A young rider in the early days, Devee Boyd, has since been a consistent help from the mechanical end. He is a local boy. His father, Ralph, works on the Taylor campus as a maintenance man, and is one of the program's unsung heroes. He has helped with the special jobs that needed doing in order to get the program rolling.

Ralph Boyd's interest in the program and Devee's interest in cycling and mechanics brought the younger man and the program together. Devee owned a Schwinn Varsity bike and though he was only fifteen at the time, he first rode with the Wheels in 1964. He was extremely strong physically and has ridden every major trip the Wheels have taken so far. To Davenport's knowledge, Devee is the only man to have cycled across the United States six times in four years. "We're pleased to think we have a man in the Wandering Wheels who is capable of doing that," Davenport says.

Devee seems to develop unusual stamina. With each crossing he appears to be in better shape physically. After completing one cross-country trip with one group of riders, he will turn right around and start off on another cross-country trip with another group of riders.

"He could literally ride circles around the other riders," remarks Davenport. "You'll see them working their guts out trying to make it to the crest of some mountain, and Devee will ride up ahead of them, turn around and coast down again, then pass them again. He physically goes beyond the call of duty."

Now at M. S. Hershey School of Medicine in Hershey, Pennsylvania, Devee continues to ride with the summer programs, keeping the guys' equipment in shape. He has become the Wheels' official mechanic.

"*. . . the Wheels' official mechanic.*"

Devee always has prided himself on being a Schwinn fan. He has always ridden his own bike, and it was he who helped change Davenport's mind in favor of the Schwinn.

6

Much of Davenport's early anxiety centered around finding the right bicycle for the program. Several months prior to the 1964 trip down the Great River Road, Davenport talked with the owner of every bicycle shop he could find. He discovered, basically, two kinds of shops: the American bike shop run by a dealer who knew little about touring and who sold mostly the popular kids' bikes; and the foreign bike dealer who could provide some good, basic information about his product, but who had no experience with touring.

Then Davenport met Gene Portuesi, a bicycle dealer from Detroit, Michigan. He published a cycling handbook and catalog which he called *Cyclo-Pedia,* and he had all kinds of equipment to sell.

Portuesi, a disciple of the European bike, not only had useful information about the foreign product, but was also an experienced rider. He himself had often raced, and he had coached the 1964 Olympic Bicycle Team. This was Davenport's first encounter with a real pro, and almost immediately he swayed Davenport toward the use of the European machine.

"They had a three-piece crank instead of the American-type one-piece crank, which, it was explained to me, was far superior," Davenport tells. "The European bike frame was put together by what was called 'lug and brazing,' which meant the bike would be much lighter than the American counterpart."

37

Davenport decided to use the French Bobet. The Louison Bobet Sports, as it was called, advertised such features as quick release, high flange alloy hubs; center pull alloy brakes; three piece cranks with machined cups and hanger axle; lugged and brazed frames built of high tensile steel tubing; and a fifteen-speed derailleur, more commonly called "gears." The frame was available in five sizes — from 20½ inches to 24½ inches — which meant that Davenport could purchase a bike according to a rider's size. The wheel sizes were the same: 27 inches. Completely equipped the bikes each weighed twenty-seven pounds.

All this seems insignificant to the novice, but to Davenport, who was looking for a quality yet low-cost bike to move his riders across thousands of miles and all kinds of terrain, it was highly impressive.

As mentioned before, Davenport drove up to Detroit in his newly acquired 1947 Chevrolet pickup truck in May of 1964 and picked up twenty-four of the Bobets for his first bicycle tour. Though the bikes retailed at $85, he was able to get them for $65 each. The bikes were painted various metallic colors, and as Davenport drove back to Upland and Taylor University, he felt some pride.

During those first two years of cycling, the Wheels encountered only a few troubles. The bikes held up well for the thousand-mile trips. The biggest problem was that the riders were Americans, not Europeans, and there is a vast difference in the way Americans handle a bike. "Our guys are brutes," says the Wandering Wheels director.

The inexperienced riders treated their bikes the same way they had treated their bikes when youngsters. While the Bobet held up for the shorter trips, Davenport began to question whether they would hold out for a longer jaunt.

Another problem was that the European bike came without kick stands. Davenport had first wanted to add the stand to each bike, but was talked out of it by Portuesi. He advised that it would only add weight to the bike and suggested that the riders just follow the example of Europeans who lean their equipment against a tree or wall when they stop to rest.

He also showed Davenport how European cyclists on tour had devised a way of stacking their bikes against each other, similar to the way rifles are stacked in the military. Davenport took the advice and decided to hold down the weight and the expense. But the riders never did learn how to stack the bikes properly, and often the whole line of bikes would crash to the ground like so many dominos. Before the second trip, the bikes were equipped with kickstands.

"We learned a lot those first years about bikes," he says. "We met some real pros along the way who prejudiced our thinking in support of the European bike. So in 1965 we continued with the Bobet."

But as Davenport continued to talk with people in the business about the kind of equipment needed for his program, he began to change his thinking. There was the influence of Devee Boyd, and to this was added that of a Schwinn dealer in Lima, Ohio.

Charlie the bike man talked seriously with Davenport about the American-built bike. "He did some outfitting of cycling clubs there," Davenport says. "He impressed me as a real pro. One day as I was in his shop waiting to talk with him further, another fellow was there wanting to buy a certain piece of equipment. Charlie wouldn't sell it to him. He told the man that it just wouldn't do the job he wanted it for. I liked this frank kind of attitude. I felt Charlie was the kind of guy I could trust."

Charlie convinced Davenport that he should contact the Schwinn Bicycle Company's general office in Chicago to talk over the possibility of using an American-built bike for the Wheels' first cross-country trip.

By this time Davenport felt that the American bike was at least as good as the European bike, and perhaps better when it came to being handled by American kids. "I came away from that shop impressed that if we could use the Schwinn, we would be money ahead as far as maintenance and efficiency were concerned." There was also the advantage of having a Schwinn dealer close by, in Gas City, Indiana.

Charlie had given Davenport the name of Al Fritz, who then was vice president of the Schwinn company. Davenport contacted Fritz, who referred him to Keith Kingbay, activities manager for the company. Kingbay travels around the country setting up bike clubs and working with park districts in developing riding and mechanic clinics and establishing bike trails. He was knowledgeable in what Davenport was trying to do as far as touring was concerned.

This was 1966, two years after Davenport had launched his Wandering Wheels program. By this time he was convinced he had a good thing going. He felt cocky enough to think that the Schwinn company might feel it a privilege to donate the bikes Davenport would need for his first cross-country trip.

He approached the company loaded for bear. He took along a portfolio with pictures of the first two trips and felt he had a good pitch.

The response from Schwinn was just the opposite of what Davenport had expected, however. "They seemed impressed with the fact that we planned to ride across the U.S. that next summer, but they didn't seem to care whether we used their bikes or not. In fact, we were told rather indirectly that Schwinn did not go out of its way to promote their bikes as much as they did cycling. They felt that they would get their fair share of the sales market that way."

Kingbay agrees. "We were interested in the Wandering Wheels," he says, "and we were ready to help them with their program. But at the time it seemed that Davenport was still grasping. Even though we didn't give Davenport what he wanted, we were in accord with what he was trying to do."

Since that first meeting, Davenport and Kingbay have become great friends and Davenport has learned to appreciate the company's sincere principles and conservative business stance. At the time, however, Davenport not only felt that the Schwinn Bicycle Company was a bit too conservative about their business dealings but that he had failed in selling his program.

Schwinn did give Davenport one Super Sport to try out on the tour and sufficient repair parts for the trip. They also offered to send the program's mechanic, Devee Boyd, to their mechanics' clinic. Davenport accepted the gifts gratefully.

By now he was nearly convinced that the Schwinn bike was what his program needed. The Super Sport and many of the parts, including the rims, were basically of European design. The crank, though one piece, was well-engineered.

Whether to buy the more expensive Schwinns or to stay with the Bobets for the first cross-country trip had to be decided. After taking inventory and talking it over with others directing the program, Davenport decided to stick with the Bobet. So for a third consecutive year, and for the first coast-to-coast bicycling trip, the Wandering Wheels were mounted upon a European bike.

Psychologically, the equipment of the Wandering Wheels is very important. "Young people are impressed with equipment," says Davenport. "They're impressed with its power, its colors, its paint job, you name it. As a result we've always been sensitive to having a little bit of class in our equipment. If need be, the Wandering Wheels will go out of its way to give its equipment a little bit of a flair."

In addition to the bicycles, other kinds of equipment are necessary to the Wandering Wheels program. The trailer, as uninteresting as it may seem, is perhaps the program's most important piece of equipment.

Early in the program Davenport realized he needed a trailer that could serve as kind of a "rolling locker room." During the two preliminary trips, the riders had brought along their personal items in a suitcase or duffle bag. These would be carried on the floor of the truck, and if anyone wanted to get something from his pack, he would first have to search it from the pile, and would then have to find what he needed in the pack. The process wasted a great deal of time.

"You can't believe how miserable it is to try to find the mate to a particular sock in the bottom of a duffle bag," Davenport explains. "We thought of various ways to solve the problem, but learned that even if we provided a hook for each bag, the riders still would be left with the problem of finding things in it."

Davenport and George spent their Christmas vacations in 1965 thinking out a design for a new-type trailer — one that would solve such problems. They knew they would need a locker arrangement, one for each rider, space for storage, and a galley that would be ready at any time.

Early the next year Davenport ordered a fourteen-foot trailer frame from Heckaman Industries, Inc. in Nappanee, Indiana. He also ordered forty aluminum lockers. Each locker would be about two feet deep; each door, twenty by twenty inches. The frame cost the program $75; the lockers would total $300 to $400.

When Davenport went to pick up the lockers, he met Mr. Hecka-man. The company owner was so impressed with what Davenport was doing that he wrote "NC" on the bill — "no charge."

"I don't know if you can catch the significance of this," Davenport says when he retells the story, "but we were not in very good shape financially. When a man like this, who really had no special reason to do so, does you a $400 favor, it makes your day a little brighter. The thing that continually impresses me in the Wandering Wheels program is that God seems to always come through when you're in need of something."

By this time Dale Murphy had signed on with the Wandering Wheels, and he offered to put the trailer together. This trailer would be the first of its kind, a Wandering Wheels trailer that allowed each rider his personal locker, which he could open with a key from the roadside, get what he needed quickly, and return to his bike. The riders could keep everything in their lockers: dry clothing, cameras, candy, money, sleeping bags. Some guys would put pictures of their girls on the insides of the doors.

The kitchen in the rear would have a large door to permit easy access to food supplies. The kitchen utensils would hang from hooks on the walls. The storage area would be large enough for all other equipment and parts.

Murf spent several nights and days working on the trailer, try-ing to put it together without any plans. He knew only that he had to put twenty doors on each side of the trailer and a kitchen in the rear. He finished it just a few days before he had to haul it out to California.

Earlier that same year, 1966, Davenport had been asked by a Chevrolet dealer in Hartford City, Indiana, to speak to the local basketball players who had just lost their tournament. They were kind of low and Bill Cooper, the car dealer, wanted Davenport to pep them up. Davenport agreed to speak at the banquet, and when Cooper asked him how much he charged for speaking, Davenport told him that if he would have the guys donate $10 toward a tent he needed for the Wandering Wheels program, that would be great.

Cooper hadn't heard of the Wandering Wheels program before,

but he was impressed with what Davenport told him about it. On the appointed day Davenport drove to Hartford City and spoke to the basketball team in a little restaurant. After the meeting Cooper presented Davenport with a twelve-by-twelve-foot, $140 tent. He had collected the money from the local Lions Club.

Later that spring Cooper helped Davenport obtain a new Chevrolet truck to haul his trailer. He worked through the central office and came up with a bright yellow half-ton pickup on loan. He made similar arrangements when Davenport needed a truck in 1967 and again in 1968. The Wheels have since purchased a three-quarter ton truck with a special bed.

As Dale Murphy set out toward California in late May in the new, yellow Chevrolet truck, he hauled a newly-painted trailer he had built bearing the sign: *Coast to Coast.*

7

"...into the surf arm in arm."

On the threshold of the summer of 1966, thirty-five young men arrived in San Francisco by jet and rendezvoused at the Covenant Church in Redwood City. They were about to embark on an adventure never before attempted by so large a group.

On June 1 they were trucked twenty miles to the ocean. There, at Half Moon Bay, the young men with Davenport and three other staff members filled a plastic gallon jug with Pacific Ocean water and set out on their grueling trip across America on bikes.

Each man rode his own Louison Bobet Sports fifteen-speed cycle, imported from France. During those twenty miles back to Redwood City, the riders encountered their first hardship — the foothills. The short ride wore off some rough edges, but also stirred some apprehension about the thirty-six-hundred-mile trip ahead.

The next morning the cyclists set out on the first leg of their journey — nine-thousand-foot-high Carson Pass in the Sierra Nevadas. Hopefully, six weeks later the young men would splash into the Atlantic Ocean at Rehoboth Beach, Delaware. Along the way they would visit such well-known American cities as Reno, Salt Lake City, Laramie, Kansas City, St. Louis, Indianapolis, Columbus, and Washington, D.C. When they reached the Atlantic they would ceremoniously pour the jug of Pacific water into the surf, symbolically ending their journey.

The trip was carefully planned. Davenport had decided on

45

". . . about to embark on an adventure never before attempted. . . ."

what seemed to be the most direct route, following old U.S. Highway 40 and the Interstate. It appeared there would not be too many serious deserts or rugged mountains on this trip.

The riders were highly disciplined and were commended by nearly every state patrolman they met along the way for complying with all safety practices and obeying rules of the road.

For safety purposes, the men rode in groups of five or six with one veteran rider as leader of each group. The groups started at regular, well-spaced intervals, and each rider was equipped with an antenna topped by an iridescent orange pennant and an iridescent orange patch for his back.

The group was followed by the specially-designed and constructed Wandering Wheels equipment and chow trailer. A sign

46

on the rear of the trailer cautioned approaching motorists: *Warning! 35 Bikes!*

This haul across America would prove to be the most extensive and the most rewarding tour to date in the Wandering Wheels program.

Some fifteen of the cyclists were Taylor students; one came from the University of Toledo; the others were either Taylor graduates or high school students from the Midwest.

Every morning after breakfast, the boys broke up into groups of six for a time of inspiration. To the cyclists, the morning Bible studies would become a high point of the trip. By 6:30 they were on the road for their daily one-hundred-mile ride.

Dale Murphy, the administrator for the trip, rode scout on a 90cc Honda motorcycle. Murf did his usual job of securing camp sites, looking up supplies, and alerting townspeople to the approach of the riders.

A tight schedule permitted only a brief lunch break. The cyclists then rode to their camp site. After supper they sang around a campfire until time to bed down. Then it was up again the next morning for breakfast.

" . what seemed to be the most direct route, . . ."

"Those first few days, from the Pacific to Carson Pass, proved to be rough."

Those first few days, from the Pacific to Carson Pass, proved to be rough. But the riders proved to be rougher. Even so, descending the Sierras came as a great relief after the nine-thousand-foot climb. And coasting downhill wasn't without its excitement. At one point the cyclists coasted thirty-five miles, reaching speeds of up to sixty-three miles per hour!

Through Nevada, Utah and Wyoming the Wheels viewed breathtaking scenery as they pedaled along the five-thousand-foot mountain plateau. And in Utah they witnessed mirages as they crossed the scorching salt flats.

Strong tail winds brought the thirty-five cyclists to Denver six days ahead of schedule. The Mile-High City was the cyclists' first long stop after leaving Half Moon Bay thirteen hundred miles back, two weeks earlier.

"We early discovered that churches provide a home away from home, wherever we are on tour," Davenport says.

Judson Memorial Baptist Church in Denver canceled its youth activities that Sunday night so the Wandering Wheels could report on its trip. Each young man appeared in his dress outfit — black slacks, white shirt, black tie.

Ben Lester, the state collegiate wrestling champ from Taylor, led the male chorus. George Smith played his guitar and sang folk songs.

Following a brief talk by Davenport, in which he explained the group's purpose, the team's skilled mechanic, Devee Boyd, explained the equipment. After the evening service, the church people treated the riders to a chicken dinner. The next day two church members loaned the boys their station wagons, so they could do some sightseeing on four wheels instead of two.

The experience of arriving nearly a week early in Denver pointed out one of the group's continuing headaches. They soon learned that it was impossible to accurately schedule a long-distance bicycle trip. At first the team tried to stay on schedule, but they soon discovered there were too many variables in weather, travel conditions, and the personal needs of thirty-five cyclists.

Denver proved to be a turning point for the Wheels as far as keeping on a rigid daily schedule. West of Denver there had been little civilization, so there was only one thing to do — ride.

An earlier breakfast quickly gave way to a 6 A.M. meal. But even allowing the riders to sleep later never made it hard for them to hit the sack.

Camp chores, clean up and Bible study continued until 8 A.M. Then the riders started off for their ride for the day.

Now the truck and trailer generally stayed with the riders all day, driving ten or fifteen miles ahead and parking along the highway. After a rest stop, the riders would get back on their bikes and the truck would drive ahead another ten or fifteen miles.

The rest stops gave each rider several chances during the day to get into his locker for whatever he needed. It also kept the truck close enough to swing back and deliver tires, tubes, or other parts for breakdowns along the way.

Murf, on the Honda, usually was the last to leave town. He would take care of last-minute details such as mail, various errands for the riders, telephone calls — and he usually didn't pass the riders until after twelve noon.

By afternoon the group had some idea where they would stop for supper. Murf would take off ahead to find a place to camp and cleanup, to buy bargain groceries, and generally to spread the word that the Wandering Wheels would be singing after supper.

Late in the day the riders were well spread out, the stronger riders keeping a lead over those who were not so well conditioned. As they pedaled through some towns, people often assumed they were in some kind of race. "Hurry up," they'd shout. "The others are way ahead."

Other people along the route were interested in the iridescent pennants flying from the antenna attached to each man's bike. The pennants, and the bright "tailpatch" of the same material, worn as an apron in reverse, had proved useful in giving approaching drivers fair warning of the slow-moving bikes.

One chubby rider had painted an official-looking "Caution — Wide Load" on his tail patch. Another rider, born of missionary parents in China, had decorated his patch with an artistic collection of Chinese characters. This became one of the groups most hilarious standing jokes. The young man would interpret the characters to the curious along the way, but each interpretation was totally different and less probable than the preceding one.

As the riders reached Kansas, they encountered the toughest sustained agony of their entire tour. From border to border they bucked forty-mile-an-hour southeast headwinds — the first two days in a dust storm.

Temperatures in Kansas ranged from 105 degrees in the day to 90 degrees at night. Only one day did the cyclists have relief from the dry heat, and that day the temperature plunged to 40 degrees, and it poured. As compensation, the Kansans were the most enthusiastic and hospitable people on the trip.

It was also in Kansas that one of the riders, Larry Witte, adopted a wild skunk which he found in Beloit. He named the skunk Ollie and raised him on a bottle. Ollie became a real camp mascot and lived in the back of the pick-up.

Because Ollie never had been deskunked, there was always the feeling that the group was carrying around a hand grenade with

50

the pin pulled. There was one close call in Richmond, Indiana, where the riders were singing to a group of summer school students in the Earlham College gym. Ollie was wandering aimlessly, as was his fashion, when suddenly a dog wandered into the gym. There was one tense moment before someone was able to grab the dog.

Near the end of the trip in Washington, D.C., the Wandering Wheels stopped two days to sing in several churches and to recuperate from the trail food. Then on Monday, July 18, they rode off toward Rehoboth Beach, Delaware, with their gallon jug of Pacific Ocean water. The trip was nearly over.

But the Wheels' problems were not over. In fact the group's completion of the trip was threatened when they reached the Chesapeake Bay Bridge. There they were told of a regulation which banned non-motorized vehicles from crossing. Not wanting to wade across the bay, the group gained permission from the Governor of Maryland, then J. Millard Tawes, to cross on state maintenance trucks.

Two days later the Wandering Wheels reached the Atlantic.

"When we saw the ocean, many of us had tears in our eyes," Davenport recalls. "I told the guys that if anyone ran ahead and touched the ocean before anyone else, he would be kicked in the pants. This was a very emotional moment for us all. I felt it

"When we saw the ocean, many of us had tears in our eyes."

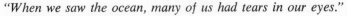

51

would only be right to make this final act a team effort, so we marched down to the beach and into the surf arm in arm."

Somehow, the riders seemed disappointed after the pouring ceremony was over. "I don't know," Davenport tries to explain, "Even though we knew it was chemically impossible, I guess some of us expected the water to explode or bubble or something. . . ."

The Wandering Wheels realized, however, and perhaps more so at this point, that God works in more quiet ways. He had worked His miracles in the lives of the thirty-five young men and the actual pouring of the Pacific Ocean water into the Atlantic Ocean turned out to be rather anti-climactic.

Back in the nation's capital, two days of concerts climaxed the thirty-six-hundred-mile cycling tour. Their final official act was to present a half-hour concert on the steps of the Capitol at the request of Congress.

Was the trip worth it?

"Man, yes!" says Dale Murphy. "It was the most valuable effort I had ever been associated with. The leadership constantly praised God for the chance to be busy at essentials for a change.

"The trip was also the most significant experience of my Christian life to that point. The extreme ranges of experience, conditions, opportunities, daily contacts, the wide contexts of life out on the road didn't allow for any 'Ivory Tower' considerations of our convictions — they had to be real to make any difference.

"As was our aim, we found ourselves considering everything, all aspects of the problem of living through twenty-four hours of God's provision. Theological niceties were practically unknown, partly because the guys were not overly conversant with the language of the church and partly because there is something essentially very unreal about a lot of theological theories.

"There was something so essentially real about the whole trip. One guy told me, 'What you believe *does* make a difference. And if it doesn't make a difference in how you live or act or think, then you really don't believe it.' I guess you'd say the greatest thing I learned that summer was how great it was to live what I said I believed. I had never had that experience before."

The effectiveness with which the Wandering Wheels achieved its spiritual goal could be seen in a variety of ways. For one, the

52

group was fused into a single organic unit by the end of the third week. The individual members recognized the selfishness and futility of an "each-for-himself philosophy." Together, they worked as a unit to achieve common goals.

Still another proof of the Wandering Wheels' effectiveness can be summed up in the reaction of the people who came in contact with the riders on the 1966 trip. A Denver newspaper noted: "This unusual group of young people isn't out to raise money. They're not toting picket signs or protesting anything. They're

". . . a deeper meaning to their relationship to each other."

just bike riders, wheeling an average of one hundred miles a day across the nation, and teaching Christ through bikes."

A reporter for a Kansas newspaper wrote this: "This group of young Christians . . . ride, swim, sing, explore, and demonstrate a tough competent manhood that is a challenge to thousands of people enroute. They will grow in stature and spirit, grow into men whom God can trust."

Through the 1966 tour, the riders gained a new perspective in their personal idea of the bigness and greatness of their Creator. They found a deeper meaning to their relationship to each other. And they discovered that Christians don't have to be the world's dull people; Christians can have something — a quality of life — that will shake the world and make it take notice.

"This trip was double everything we had anticipated," says Murf. "It was twice the work, twice the fun, twice the agony, and twice the growth and accomplishment."

This third Wandering Wheels excursion once again confirmed for Davenport that his program was something young people needed. It was filling the adventure gap with challenge and excitement. "It was becoming apparent," he says, "that there is something real and vital about the salt and sweat and rugged terrain and demanding pace. When a young man feels that thrill deep down inside at being part of a disciplined, vitally masculine group of God's men, I think Wandering Wheels has begun to accomplish its purpose. It is then that young men are on their way to a more clear and deep and vital relationship to their God."

8

"It must be the Hell's Angels!"

On its initial cross-country trip, the Wandering Wheels discovered that the bikes, being inexpensive, caused some embarrassment. As they rode into towns along the way, they would meet bike enthusiasts who took the occasion to inform the Wheels just what was wrong with the equipment they were using. Many of these bike bugs rode $250 hand-tooled European machines with all kinds of expensive gadgetry — special hubs, special rims, special seats, even special water bottles. All the Wheels had needed was a bicycle that could carry them down the highway 100 to 120 miles a day.

Despite the aggravation of receiving unsought criticism and advice of this nature, Davenport looked upon the experience as valuable, because it introduced him to the ultra in the bike world. And there was one consolation the young riders had over their enthusiastic critics: with their meager piece of machinery, they were doing what no one else had ever had the guts to do before. They had a program that was giving them an experience that none of their critics ever had with their fancy equipment.

Apart from this kind of criticism, the Wandering Wheels were coming to some decisive conclusions about the future of the European bike in the program. As they pedaled from town to town, state to state, the bikes were taking a terrible beating. "Oh, they took us across the U.S. without one total breakdown," Davenport confirms, "but they were in too poor shape to use the following year. We recognized that we were going to have to buy new ones.

"It would be unfair to leave the impression that the European rig had not been good," says Davenport. "It served the Wandering Wheels well for each of the three tours for which we purchased them. Remember that there was one main reason for looking at another bike for the program: the need to withstand the hard treatment by inexperienced American cyclists."

There was another fact to be considered: The Schwinn is sturdier because it is heavier; it weighs twenty-nine pounds compared to the other's twenty-seven pounds. In addition, the Schwinn costs a great deal more than the foreign bike: the Super Sport retails for about $125; the other retails for $85. Even with the "discount" given the Wandering Wheels by the Schwinn company, the Wheels had to increase its output of funds for the Schwinn. As Davenport puts it: "The European rig gave us all we could expect from it."

Following the first cross-country trip, Davenport went back to the Schwinn company to see Kingbay.

"We still felt he had a tremendous program," says Kingbay. "He was not only promoting cycling, but he was giving an image to American young people that we liked. We're flag-wavers at Schwinn; we're proud of America; we're fed up with the kind of young people who want to destroy this country.

"We were impressed with the calibre of youth Davenport took with him on these trips, and the positive image they were producing. The program was good for young people and cycling both."

Davenport made arrangements to purchase the Schwinn bikes he would need for his 1967 crossing for a price suitable to both parties.

"The Schwinn has since proved to be the bike for the Wandering Wheels," Davenport says. "It has the guts to withstand the abuse of the typical American youth."

Many of the parts on the Schwinn Super Sport, now the Wandering Wheels' official bike, are built in Europe, yet they are sturdier and more expensive than similar parts on the European machine. Though the Schwinn has only ten speeds, the gears cover as wide a range as those on the fifteen-speed bikes. The one-piece crank contains a much larger bearing which can take the more rugged workout by American cyclists.

". . . . guts to withstand the abuse. . . ."

". . . the small pest."

Like the European bike, the Schwinn comes in various frame sizes. So the Schwinn, too, could be "custom made" for each Wandering Wheels rider. The Super Sport model comes in a 19-inch, 22-inch, or 24-inch frame size. Like the foreign rig, the Schwinn is equipped with 27-inch-wheels.

In 1967 Davenport purchased eighty Schwinn Super Sports. Each was painted metallic blue, a favorite Wandering Wheels color, and each was equipped with the best premium bike tires available.

At first, the riders encountered some troubles with their new bikes. "The kids were always putting too much air in their tires," explains Davenport. "As a result, they were blowing them out. We — the Wandering Wheels program — were footing the bill for the parts, and each tire cost a $1.25, so we began to put the screws to the guys, threatening them with K.P. or some other chore."

A second problem the riders encountered came in the form of a tiny thistle. Davenport has never seen this thistle, which the people out West call a "goathead thistle," in the East. It looks much like a burr, and it has a sticker just long enough to puncture the tire, creating a slow leak.

One morning the Wheels woke up to find that twenty of the tires were flat. From then on the Wheels were on the look-out for the small pest. In the meantime, they bought some gunk to seal the inside of the tires against small punctures.

The sealer really moved the Wheels along, because previously they had experienced four or five flats a day from these thistles. (The record number of flats by one rider on one trip is seventeen.)

With the Wandering Wheels officially mounted on Schwinns in 1967, Davenport began seriously to consider an additional mode of transportation for himself. He wasn't about to ride a bicycle across America a second time.

"Not that I didn't want to ride a bike across again," he is quick to explain. "I just wanted to be able better to direct the program while it was in action."

For this reason, Davenport purchased a Triumph 500cc motorcycle for $1,200.

It had not originally been his plan to rely upon a motorcycle in the Wandering Wheels program, but in those first two years of Wandering Wheels, Davenport felt that a motorcycle might be used to run errands for the group. Hence, on the Wheels 1966 cross-country trip, recall, Dale Murphy rode along on a Honda 90cc. The spirited machine proved to be useful. As a result, the motorcycle became an integral part of the Wandering Wheels program after that first cross-country trip.

And so it was that Davenport bought the larger motorcycle for use on the two 1967 crossings. Not only did it affirm its usefulness, but the motorcycle offered some extra glamor to the program.

"The kids in the towns we rode through were greatly attracted by the motorcycle," Davenport explains. "And we found that even the bike riders took a little extra pride in the program. Of course, they were always eager for a chance to ride the motorcycle as a form of recreation."

This appeal began to reveal to Davenport that perhaps the motorcycle could also be a valuable tool for attracting young people. Remember that his original intent in getting a group of young kids riding bikes was to reach them on a level on which he could communicate with them. What the bicycle had done already seemed to be pointing the founder and director of the Wandering Wheels toward what the motorcycle could do.

During the 1967 tours Davenport learned several skills on his motorcycle. It allowed him to leave the group early in the afternoon to arrange for a place to stay. This advantage, of course, had been proved the year before when Murf rode a motorcycle.

Davenport would rumble into town about mid-afternoon wearing his riding helmet, jacket, levis, and boots, looking the part of the motorcyclist. He'd tell the town leader that he was riding a motorcycle across America and escorting forty kids on bikes.

In some towns, he found he looked too much the part. Immediately when he'd announce he was leading forty cyclists and wanted to spend the night, he'd see fear strike the faces of many. It was as if they were thinking: "Forty cyclists! It must be the Hell's Angels!"

Davenport, knowing why the people were reacting in this manner, would try to explain that he was leading *bicycle* riders, not motorcycle riders. But even so, there would be occasions when he would be standing near a mayor as the riders filed into town and hear him exclaim, "Oh, they're on bicycles."

The motorcycle also proved to be part of the Wheels' safety program. Davenport learned quickly that one way to hold down

"It must be the Hell's Angels!"

"Both Davenport and Murf rode the pack."

accidents is to make sure each rider is constantly being observed. With someone in the pack watching him, a rider will be extra careful in obeying the rules of the road. Somehow the fear of being chewed out by Davenport or one of the other leaders carries more weight than the possibility of a collision.

"The riders might be spread out as much as twenty miles apart," says Davenport. "I could use the motorcycle to ride back and forth from pack to pack, checking up on them."

As Murf had learned in 1966, the motorcycle could also be used effectively to take care of business matters without holding up the riders. In 1967 Davenport would stay back in a town after the last group of riders would head out for the day and telephone back to Upland to report on the status of the program. Then he would phone ahead to make arrangements for a place to stay that night. The whole process, including taking care of the mail and buying personal items for the riders, would take forty-five minutes to an hour. By then, the riders could be a good fifteen to twenty miles down the road.

In 1968 the Wheels purchased two of the Triumph motorcycles. Both Davenport and Murf rode the pack. Then in 1969 Davenport met a Harley-Davidson salesman, Duane Unkefer of Milwaukee, Wisconsin, who loaned him one Harley Sportster 900cc for the tour from Miami, Florida, to Seattle, Washington. Davenport also purchased a 1961 police motorcycle — a three-wheeler — and spruced it up with $1,000 worth of chrome and accessories. It was a real eyecatcher!

"To this day I can remember pulling into an A & W Root Beer stand and watching the reaction of some of the kids. A lot of the guys were there in their fancy GTO's showing off their sophistication. When our guys rode in on their bicycles, a few of the kids got out of their cars and wandered over to find out what the riders were doing. The supersophisticates, however, stayed in their cars.

"When I roared in on my Sportster, followed by our fancy three-wheel job all do-daddied up, it wasn't long before they were all out of their cars asking us all kinds of questions."

That was exactly the response for which Davenport was looking. He was convinced that h᠈ had found another tool to aid in communicating with young people. The years ahead would prove whether he was right.

The first hand-built trailer went across America three times — once in 1966 and twice in 1967. But it took just three trips to prove that a number of things needed to be done to improve it. Instead of trying to rebuild the original trailer, Davenport decided to build a new one.

The Wandering Wheels went all out. About three-quarters of the trailer would be commercially built. Davenport went to Wells Cargo, Inc. in Elkhart, Indiana, and purchased a longer trailer frame: a seventeen-foot frame compared to the former fourteen-foot one.

It still had to have the custom work done to it, like putting in the lockers, installing the kitchen in the back, and adding lights around it. A custom door was fitted to the rear so that the Wandering Wheels cooks could serve from inside. All this made the new trailer a "Cadillac" compared to the one they were used to.

The most impressive experience associated with the new trailer took place after the unit was assembled and painted. Proud of the piece of equipment they had put together, Davenport wasn't about to spare the horses on a new stove and grill. He would go all out for the best.

On the original trailer the stove had been inefficient in the higher altitudes. The cook always had difficulty getting the food heated up quickly. To help solve the problem, Davenport went looking for the biggest stove and largest grill he could get.

He went to a company in South Bend, Indiana, by the name of South Bend Range Corporation, a manufacturer of restaurant-type kitchen equipment. He walked into the place less than a week away from pulling out on the '68 trip. "I just figured I could find what I needed, throw it in the truck, and head back home," he explains.

Inside, Davenport introduced himself at the information booth and asked for a salesman. The salesman came out and formally introduced himself.

Davenport told him about the Wandering Wheels and that he needed one of their stoves and a grill for his trailer galley. He gave the salesman the specifications, then said, "I'd like to take them back with me today."

"Today!" the salesman repeated. "Oh, that would be impossible. It'll take a week to ten days to have them made up for you."

Davenport didn't know what to say. He needed them that week, because the trailer would be pulling out for the West Coast before the week was over. But he still had a note of optimism as he thought about how God had led the Wheels so far, every detail working out without a hitch.

Never really ending their conversation about the Wandering Wheels program and athletics in general, the two men stood there and talked awhile. Then the salesman invited Davenport on a little tour of the company so he could see its wares. Soon they

63

approached a large stove, and Davenport remarked about it.

"How would that one do in high altitudes?" he asked the salesman.

"Man, you could boil water anywhere with this one," he said.

"Well, can't I buy this one then?" Davenport felt certain that the salesman had overlooked the unit and would agree to sell it.

"No. We built this one to order for the Colonel Sanders chicken outfit," the salesman answered. "See?" He pointed to a name plate on the front of the range.

Davenport was certain that this was just the stove they needed. It had three large burners and looked like it could heat up an entire building. But the salesman stood firm, then led him on to where they were making the grills.

Upon walking into the area, Davenport observed a large man dressed in bib overalls, a big union button pinned to one of the straps. As the employee was lifting a large twenty-by-thirty-inch grill, the salesman beckoned to him. "What do you think?" he asked the man, "How long would it take to get one of these ready?"

"Oh, a little over a week, I'd guess," the man in overalls answered. Davenport felt sick.

Just about then the man stopped what he was doing and turned. "What size do you need?"

Davenport told him.

"You know," he said to the salesman, "I don't know whose mistake it was, but we made two like that last week for a customer, and he had ordered only one." He pointed to a crate. "We made one too many."

There, leaning against the wall, was the exact piece of equipment Davenport needed. It was all boxed up with metal bands strapped around it, all ready to go.

But Davenport still needed a stove. "Well, what about that stove?" he asked the salesman. By that time the salesman must have caught the spirit of the moment, for he went and found a screw driver and led Davenport back to the stove. Taking the name plate off and tossing it in the corner, he said, "That's not a Colonel Sanders unit any more," and Davenport agreed. A few minutes later both units were loaded in the truck and Davenport was ready to head back toward Upland.

Davenport went back in to pay the bill, which came to $400, and about that time the head salesman for the company walked in. He heard the story about the Wheels, and how Davenport had come in for this equipment, and how it was supplied "miraculously" in just a few short moments.

The head man had just returned from an urban renewal meeting, which had been up to its neck in problems, and when he heard this story, it rang a note of good news. As he took the bill, which he had to okay, he wrote, "NC," — no charge — across the bottom and told Davenport to tear up his check.

Davenport pulled out of town hardly able to contain himself. "I almost felt like I'd run into a room and seen God," he says. "I had to tell people about this."

On another occasion he was looking for blinker safety lights — the kind you see on construction sites along the highway. The lights stand about ten inches high. Below sits a box to house the battery. The light itself is about four inches in diameter. He had noticed that the Amish people used them on their horse-drawn carriages to warn cars of their slow-moving vehicles, and he felt that the Wandering Wheels could use some in case of an emergency.

Davenport knew of an Amish supply store in Middlebury, Indiana, and one day decided to stop on his way to Grand Rapids, Michigan. Sure enough, when he went into the store he found what he was looking for. But he discovered that each would cost more than fourteen dollars.

"I wanted to provide safety for these kids in case they had to ride at night," Davenport explains, "so I decided I would buy them at that price."

But — you guessed it — as Davenport was about to pay for $150 worth of blinking safety lights, the owner walked in. When Davenport told him how he was going to use them, the store owner revealed he had been a trustee at Taylor University formerly and had heard of the Wandering Wheels program. He gave the lights to him.

By the time the 1968 cross-country trip was to begin, the Wandering Wheels leaders had little doubt that it would get off smoothly. There was one hurdle yet to overcome. Julian Gromer, the professional travelogue photographer who had asked to document the trip on film, requested only one thing from the Wheels. He asked that he be provided with a convertible car, so he could easily film the trip while it was in motion.

Roger Demarest had ridden on the Wheels' 1966 trip. His father, a car dealer in Westwood, New Jersey, consented to loan a convertible.

"We needed to put the car in our name for the crossing," Davenport tells. "We had to pick up our license tag for the car, too. So we sent off a guy who was going on our '68 trip to pick up the car, and we told him we would send him the license plates so he could drive it back."

When Bobby Wynkoop, the driver, was already on his way to Westwood to pick up the car, Davenport discovered that he could not get the plates unless the car was in the state. Even though Davenport had the title, the car needed to pass a state safety inspection before the plates could be issued. "So there I was," says Davenport, "with all I needed to get the plates except the car, and there was Bobby with the car and without the plates. I had to have the car in Indiana the next morning, but Bobby couldn't drive it without the plates."

As Davenport stepped into the license bureau's accounting area to learn if there was any solution to the dilemma, who should step from behind the counter but a part-time preacher he had met the night before. Davenport had spoken at a banquet in the preacher's church that night.

"To tell you the truth," Davenport confesses, "I hadn't been too excited about going to this man's church to speak as a has-been football player. Little did I realize that God had planned that meeting so that this man could help us out."

Davenport doesn't know how it came about, but somehow the man got the safety check waived and Davenport received the license plates. He then rushed back to the Taylor campus hoping to find a car leaving for New Jersey, for most of the students were on their way home for the summer.

Outside the campus bookstore he spotted a car with New Jersey plates being loaded. It belonged to a student's mom, but the occupants were going on a five-day vacation before returning home. Next, Davenport headed toward the dorms. There were four cars there packed ready to go.

"Anybody here going to Jersey?" Davenport shouted.

A guy in a sports car shouted back, "Yeah, I am."

"When are you leavin'?"

"As soon as I finish talking here."

"Any chance you'll be going near a place called Westwood?"

The guy looked back at Davenport. "I live two miles from that place."

The plates were on the convertible and the car on its way back the next day.

9

"It brings out the best and worst in you."

Another major obstacle that threatened the 1968 trip — in fact, the entire Wandering Wheels program — occurred on the heels of the 1967 tours. Once again Davenport was deeply concerned about the lives he was committed to handle on the highway. This is how he explains his feelings at that time:

"Appreciate the fact that most of the kids who come to us are deeply loved by moms and dads. If some kid was along whose mom and dad were always too drunk to really care, and if the kid was badly hurt or killed, the parents would probably shrug it off. But when moms and dads write and phone along the trip, you know they are concerned.

"I felt this pressure both on the 1966 and again on the two 1967 trips. I found myself feeling like a baby-sitter, particularly with the younger riders. I was living hour by hour in fear that something might happen to one or more of my charges.

"For example, in 1967 David Doud was riding ahead of me rolling into Kansas and suddenly slipped off the pavement onto the shoulder. In his attempt to get back on the pavement, he flipped off his bike and skidded onto the road. In that instant I envisioned a car or a truck coming along and hitting him. Luckily, the road was clear, and David just had a few bruises. And I think what made the incident more dramatic was that it happened just ten miles from his home.

"At the time I was not to the place where I could give God

the responsibility to care for the kids. I was really anxious for their safety. Because of my fear of what might happen, I began to think seriously that it wouldn't be completely justifiable to continue the program.

"Other times when we weren't on tour, I'd be driving along some of our two-lane highways, following a truck. The truck would hardly fit within the boundaries of the lane. Alongside the pavement, there would be a two-inch drop to the shoulder. I'd catch myself wondering how in the world I could put a kid on a bike in a situation like that.

"But, you know, once you put a bike on the road with the bright orange flag overhead and a similar patch on the rider's back, the traffic always seems to adapt. And all I had to do was to hand back these kids to their moms and dads and listen to them relate this experience to their Christian life, and that was really all the encouragement I needed to continue.

"The reason for beginning the Wandering Wheels in the first place, I reminded myself, was 'to put hair back on the church's "chest" ' and to prove that the Christian life can be a real challenging experience. After talking over my fears with my wife and others who knew the program well, I came to the reassured conclusion that the program was sound."

From then on, Davenport went full time into developing the Wandering Wheels program.

One thing about a program like the Wandering Wheels: you can be with people in a number of situations and think you know all about them, but until you are riding with them on a bike trip, you learn they aren't as you may have first imagined.

Before each trip the riders tended to put on false personalities. It wears off quickly on a cycling trip.

Before departure Davenport imagines just how certain riders will turn out during the tour. He's always guessed wrong. "I'd wind up honoring fellas I never thought I would," he concedes. "Riding the bike gives you a real life situation. It brings out the best and worst in you. All the sham and all that you take for granted is suddenly wiped out. You see each other as you really are. You learn to appreciate the other guy."

One of the early Wandering Wheels was Larry Witte. Larry

70

was a student at Taylor when he went on the 1966 tour. He since went on to Toledo University where he earned an engineering degree.

"Larry had an imaginative mind," Davenport recalls. "He was creative and could figure anything out. I remember when we broke out a new tent and couldn't figure out how to put it together, Larry came over to help us. There were a lot of odds and ends, and we had no instructions, but in about a half-hour Larry had figured it out and had the tent up.

"Larry was one of those guys I had figured wrong from the start. He hadn't impressed me too greatly before we started the trip, but it wasn't long before I was proved wrong."

Larry was also a photo hound, which gave him a good excuse to ride slowly. Davenport recalls many times when the group would leave him behind on the road, and he'd come riding into camp an hour or two late. "But he really enjoyed his riding," Davenport says.

Once, near St. Louis along the Mississippi River, Larry stopped to talk to an old native and persuaded him to give him a boat. Larry and another rider, Bill Kelly, put their bikes in the boat and drifted down the Mississippi. Davenport didn't know anything about it until later that night when they didn't show up. Then some of the other riders told Davenport what Witte and Kelly had done. That night the two riders ran out of daylight and had to pull the boat to shore and sleep in a jail cell.

Another time just out of a small town in Kansas, Larry concocted the idea of rigging a sail to his bicycle. Sure enough, the next morning he put up his sail and took off with the wind to his back. It worked well — for a while. The wind switched later that morning, and the sail knocked him off his bike.

Earlier on that trip, Larry, like every other rider, had high hopes of finding a rattle snake so he could take it home as some kind of a trophy. One night in the desert area, he came wheeling into camp — late as usual — all excited: "Hey, I've got a rattler cornered back here," he yelled.

"Where?"

"Back a ways, but I'm afraid to get him myself. Some of you guys come help me!"

When he and his band of hunters returned to the place Larry

had cornered the rattler, the snake was gone. All summer long he looked for another one, but never as much as heard another. He couldn't even find a dead one, so he could cut off the rattles to take home.

There have been a lot of "Larrys" on the Wandering Wheels trips. Many of them were "latecomers." They weren't necessarily athletic or didn't have outstanding personalities. They just liked apple pie and mom and went to church and wore average clothing. They were just average guys.

Davenport soon found he liked the "average guys" category of riders. They were the kind who would volunteer for anything. They were the ones who were always around to do the work. They were the fellas who went to bed late because they were helping a buddy fix his bike, or they were going out of their way to talk to someone at length about the trip and about their God. "Maybe my 'strongest' men were the ones who were least attractive as far as looks or personality or sociability," Davenport says. "I found this type to be the silent leaders who turned out to be the strongest personalities of the trip."

A pair of Wandering Wheels well remembered by the other riders on the 1968 tour went by the names of Grube and Small. The two were always riding together. Grube was the leader and Small the follower, so it seemed.

Jimmy Small weighed about 220 pounds, had red hair and freckles, and appeared a bit dependent. He was always losing his locker key and bothering the other riders in his embarrassed little way to borrow their keys.

Every time the group was about to head out on its next leg of the trip, if Grube and Small weren't together, you'd hear Grube going about yelling, "Smaaaallll." And Small would be wandering about yelling, "Gruuuube." As one '68 rider put it, "It sounded like a mating call."

The two were nearly inseparable, and Grube was always looking after Small. Perhaps it was a good thing. One day out in cattle country Grube came across a cattle crossing in the road bed. He spotted it first and decided to get off his bike and flag down Small so he wouldn't run across it and fall. The crossing was the type where several rails were imbedded in the road with spaces between. Cattle could not cross the section without their legs slipping between the rails. If a bike hit the crossing at the wrong angle, the tire would drop into one of the spaces.

Grube jumped off his bike and began flagging down Small so he wouldn't fall, but Small came barreling across the grate full speed. Once on the other side he jumped off his bike. "What do you want, Grube?" he said.

Another time Small was leader of his particular pack of riders. One morning they headed out before sunrise, and it wasn't until the sun came up that they realized that Small had led them back toward Miami instead of toward Seattle, their destination.

The Wheels have also included riders from backgrounds other than "Christian" — by that, meaning, other than churched. On one trip Davenport had a couple of seniors and a junior in high school from the Jersey City area who thought they were "pretty hot stuff."

At the beginning of the tour, just before taking off on the first leg, Davenport went into town to do some shopping. He quickly learned that these three fellows had been doing some "shopping" of their own.

When he entered the store, he heard the cashier say, "Hey, there's another one of them." She said it loud enough so Davenport could hear. Davenport could tell from the way she announced it that one or some of his guys wearing their Wandering Wheels jackets had done something wrong. Davenport walked over to the cashier and asked what she meant.

"Well, there were three of you fellas with jackets like that who stole a hat and a couple of apples and ate them right here." She meant they ate the apples, not the hat, and pointed to where they had dropped the cores.

Davenport got their description and got on his motorcycle and roared back to camp ready to explode. As he later put it, "This thing that I was attempting to do in the name of God was backfiring before I hardly got it off the ground."

Back at camp Davenport got a kangaroo court going and charged these kids with the stealing. "I was ready to ship them back home on the first plane," he recalls.

The trio admitted what they had done and promised to keep their records clean for the rest of the trip. They made a full apology to the store owner and paid for what they had stolen. Davenport had a lot of spade work to do on that trip.

Even in incidences like these Davenport says he feels a "strange closeness to God." He says it's hard to explain them otherwise to his satisfaction.

On one of the '69 trips Davenport had several riders from the major cities such as Philadelphia, New York, and Washington, D.C., as well as a number of guys from rural areas. Sometimes they didn't mix too well because of their conflicting life styles.

During the cross-country trip from Seattle to Washington, D.C., there had been one kid who had been a continual source of ir-ritation to many of the riders. "It wasn't completely due to his own person," Davenport says, coming to his defense. "He was a live example of a product of the environment in which he grew up.

"He just wasn't anywhere near the kind of kid he could be. He was the kind that, under normal circumstances, you would have given up on long ago. For us, it wasn't that easy — not with the type of program we run. We can't say, 'Go on; get out of here!' and dump a kid like this. We believe God gives us every kid in our program, and we weren't about to throw away a chance to work with one of them.

"This fella had a whole life of being turned away and kicked in the pants — nobody loving him. So you couldn't expect him to suddenly be somebody he wasn't."

The Wheels had rolled all the way from Seattle through Toledo and Sandusky, Ohio, and into Apple Creek before the situation came to a head. All along the way, however, there had been fights, and it seemed that this one guy was always in them, or at least the cause of them. Some of the other riders spoke of his pulling a knife on one occasion, and Davenport always lived with the fear that one of these nights something might really happen that would tarnish the tour.

In Apple Creek, Ohio, the riders were invited to spend the night in a nice country church located on a hill. It was a muggy, lazy sort of a night. The fellas had comfortably settled themselves in the church kitchen, munching on some of the extra food from the evening's banquet and talking about some of the things they had experienced so far on the trip.

74

Because the evening had been fairly in order, Davenport decided to go to bed early and get a little extra sleep. He walked around the church building looking for a quiet place to roll out his sleeping bag and found a little boiler room where he knew no one could find him and disturb him. He stretched out his foam rubber mattress and sleeping bag and laid back to go to sleep.

But for some reason he didn't feel like sleeping, and growing uneasy just lying there, he got up and began wandering around again. "Somehow I felt attracted to the kitchen; I had no particular reason for going there. I just sort of headed in that direction without giving it much thought."

But as Davenport stepped into the room, he found himself walking in on a fight that had just begun. It involved this same fellow — a high school student — and a college student. Immediately, Davenport separated the two.

"I'm going to get even!" the younger fighter shouted. "I'll never forgive you!"

The kid's reaction bothered Davenport so much that he blew his cool: "Okay, man; you're going home!"

Davenport explains what happened next: "For several weeks some of the guys had been on my back to send this kid home; I had always said No. But this time I'd had it. I told him to get his bottom out of there, and I would have his bus ticket in the morning.

"After I cooled off, however, I really didn't feel that this was the right solution. No one had really ever loved or cared or gone the second mile with this kid before. So I let things cool off for awhile."

Davenport, of course, had been left with this one attitude in mind: that the kid was going to get even one way or another and that he wasn't going to be happy until he did.

Later, the Wandering Wheels leader brought the two young men together to find out just what had precipitated the fight. Another rider on the tour, Jerry Whittington, sat in. Jerry was a graduate of Calvin College of Grand Rapids, Michigan, where he had majored in psychology and sociology. He had also worked in the Outward Bound program (a program which places young people in hardship environments in order to bring out their potential), and was knowledgeable in counseling. All four of them went off to talk together.

"The college kid was, of course, one of the riders who had been bugged by this guy on the entire trip. He was perhaps a bit too anxious to find an excuse for a scuffle," Davenport explains. "We went around and around with the problem for nearly a half-hour without seeming to get anyplace.

"Then we began talking about 'grass roots' things — about why people act the way they do, about sin, about personal guilt, about being products of the environment. Suddenly this high school kid broke down and began to cry — as a man would cry. Before long he wound up telling the other kid that he was sorry, and then the other kid, a college junior, started crying.

"Right there these two guys bawled together, and before long the two became friends. From then on the younger boy made a real effort to shape up his life. He still had some problems, but the rest of us could tell that he was trying."

Davenport feels that he was prompted to move toward the kitchen that night by God. As a result he was able to initiate a turning point in this rider's life.

10

"We want to hang loose."

When these novice riders climb aboard their bikes at the beginning of a tour, few of them have had much time for preparation. Most of them have been busy with studies right up to the time they leave, and there is little they can learn in the few months of preparation from the time they have signed on to go.

"There's only one way to get into shape to ride a bike 120 miles a day," says Davenport, "and that's to ride a bike 120 miles a day." There are, however, a few preliminary lessons.

These kids enter what may be the toughest physical test of their lives. The progress of the group will be no better than the weakest rider, and none of them wants to be that rider. Each knows that he is responsible for himself. If he doesn't do his best to fulfill some minimal requirements before the trip, the entire group will suffer. It won't take long for the group to see who is the weakest among them.

"These riders are like military recruits," says Davenport. "They're going to get into shape the first few weeks of the trip. The first few days, every part of their bodies will ache, and the part that will ache the most are what we call their 'buffies.' Sitting on that thin, leather seat for twelve hours will make them numb. They'll soon find there's nothing better than to go into a restaurant and sit down on a foam rubber pad and just ooze down into the seat, spreading their bottoms out over every available inch."

Davenport has set up a few minimum standards for physical

conditioning before the trip. Sit-ups, squat jumps, and push-ups are a must. The riders are instructed to find their maximum in all three exercises and then not be satisfied until they can increase that number by ten each. They are to work on these every other day.

"Of course we require that each rider get a checkup from his doctor before going on the trip," Davenport says. "If he's in good health, we can't hurt him."

Running is also included in the conditioning program. The riders are advised to run at least a mile every other day. If possible, the rider should attempt to stretch out his running — farther and faster as the trip gets nearer.

Moving around in this manner, or by riding their bikes or by doing other kinds of strenuous work for up to an hour, should bring about a good sweat. Bringing the heartbeat up to a good exercising load will circulate the blood and build endurance.

As soon as the riders receive their bikes, they are told to ride ten miles a day, every day. Miss a day, and they are told to make it up double. By departure time each rider should have put about five to six hundred miles on his bike — and on his body.

The riders are also warned to fight the tendency to loaf when working out and to watch their sleeping and eating habits. "Cut out the junk eats," they are told, "and get more than enough sleep. The body can develop incredible power and stamina if it has a chance to recover and rebuild."

Mentally and emotionally, the rider has to be ready for work he has never experienced before. One of the most difficult mental adjustments in the program is to withstand situations where they may be riding in one kind of environment two or three days at a time.

"In the Western states, particularly in Kansas, there is little variety," explains Davenport. "Some of our riders from the big Eastern cities can't believe how far it is from point to point. And when we bring them through Montana from the Idaho border to the Dakota border it's nearly five hundred miles. That's almost as far as it is from Taylor to New York City!

"It's like placing each of the riders on a treadmill and getting them nowhere. Same trucks. Same hills. Same everything, so it seems. For miles they see few people and few billboards. This is a tremendous emotional strain on the guys. Sometimes it's even tougher than the physical strain."

There is really no way the riders can prepare for such strain. It's the same situation with the spiritual aspects of the Wandering Wheels program. In preparing spiritually, the riders are told to come only with the amount of God they know. "Don't do us the injustice of coming with a false side of yourself," they are told. "You don't have to show off more of God than you really have."

Davenport encourages each rider to allow God to use the trip's experiences to teach them about Himself. That way, anything they take on new will be theirs. "To me," says Davenport, "one of the greatest disservices to Christendom are the people who put on a garb of Christianity without being able to back it up with reason or action."

Early in the Wandering Wheels program Davenport came up with a motto that he felt was a little catchy and used it in an attempt to explain the purpose of his program. The motto, "Teaching Christ through Bikes," appeared on the early brochures about the Wheels, and it seemed to take hold in Davenport's circles. But after a few years of spreading out with the program, he found that the motto wasn't too effective. He and the riders found they were needing to explain the motto's technical meaning, and few of them could come up with a satisfying answer.

What the motto meant, and what the Wandering Wheels program attempted to do was to teach information about Christ and the Christian life through the medium of the bicycle. "We are teaching the fact of Jesus Christ," states Davenport. "We are teaching, through daily confrontation, that Jesus was a historical person who roamed this earth some two thousand years ago, was killed, buried, and returned to life. We learn that He is very much a part of history today.

"As Christian athletes we simply believe that man's sin has separated him from God and that the only forgiveness for sin is in God's Son, Jesus Christ. We have personally discovered that this faith in Christ not only provides for eternity, but also offers satisfaction, excitement, and ultimate purpose in daily living.

"We attempt to teach through bikes how to live a purposeful, abundant life — just as Christ used the mustard seed and other

79

at-hand mediums to teach the meaning of living. The bicycle has allowed us to encounter a number of situations that could parallel things in the Bible. It has allowed us to prove God at His Word, to trust Him for a place to stay at night, for example.

"Christ had a lot to say about living life in hardship situations. In this generation where kids have sat around and experienced life only vicariously, we are giving them real experiences in which they can put themselves and the Creator of the universe to the test.

"Being a Christian is not just a one-hour-a-week exercise, but a twenty-four-hour-a-day experience. Sharing food, doing someone else's job when he's unable to do it — when you're on a bike, man, it all hangs out. You can't camouflage the real you."

The spiritual side of the program Davenport usually plays by ear. "We want to hang loose," he says. "We don't want to structure it too much. We let the riders use their good judgment, knowing that they are under constant surveillance by their peers and by the people they meet."

As mentioned earlier, with the exception of maybe one or two riders on each tour, the majority of Wandering Wheels have had no experience with bicycle touring. In addition, an equal majority have had little or no experience with the use of a derailleur lightweight bike. While such equipment is strong and rugged, it is possible for the careless or inexperienced rider to damage his bike. The brutality with which the early Wandering Wheels riders handled their bikes, as you will recall, was a principle cause for switching to the slightly heavier American bicycle.

But even the American club-type bicycles, like the Schwinns used by the Wandering Wheels, are designed for travel and must be handled properly in order to give good service. The riders are instructed not to run over curbs, rocks, into walls or other immovable objects, nor across sharp edged holes. Properly handled, the bikes will negotiate the roughest terrain, safely and speedily.

The derailleur gear, properly used, is extremely rugged and will last for many years of hard service. Its operating principle differs from that of the hub or three-speed gear. If the differences are understood, the rider will find the derailleur to be a strong, extremely versatile, serviceable assistant in hillclimbing and in riding against headwinds. Improperly handled, the rider can inflict on his bike bent forks, frame, rims, and damaged tires. Poorly coordinated gear shifting can result in a bent or damaged gear, chain, and sprockets.

For these reasons, the Wandering Wheels rider should spend as much time as possible getting acquainted with his bike before the trip begins. The frame size of the bike has been carefully selected to fit each rider. With the proper size bike, the rider should be able to straddle the bicycle's horizontal bar just enough to place both his feet flat on the ground when in stocking feet. A too small bike will not permit a proper setting of the saddle (seat) or the handlebars.

Because the bicycle utilizes nearly all the body muscles, failure to acquire a proper fit will cause unnecessary discomfort, premature fatigue, and poor control. A proper fit, on the other hand,

"The derailleur gear . . . extremely rugged. . . ."

will give the rider maximum efficiency in his riding, no matter what the conditions.

The height of the saddle is also of prime importance. To check the adjustment, each rider sets the crank (to which the pedal is attached) so that one of the pedals is in its lowest position. He then sits on the seat and places the ball of his foot on the low pedal. His leg should be almost straight while sitting in this position. Not to have the saddle in proper position is to be unable to take full advantage of the leg muscles while pedaling.

The Wandering Wheels' bikes are equipped with underslung handlebars, which, when properly fitted, permit better body weight distribution for stability and ease of propulsion. This type of dropped handlebar, with which most derailleur bicycles are fitted, permits the rider's spine to relax as he bends forward. This allows easier breathing, aids in absorbing road shock, and reduces wind resistance. The top of the handlebar is set no higher than the saddle top. When in proper position, the handlebars permit the rider's back to position in an approximate 45-degree angle.

At first the riders find the riding position strange, and many feel some discomfort in their neck and wrist muscles. However, it isn't long before their bodies adjust to the situation.

Once fitted to his bike, the Wandering Wheels rider is ready to road test his equipment. He must get used to the positioning of his body, the use of the brake levers, which are mounted on the top of the handlebars, and the use of the derailleur gears. Part of Davenport's insistence that the riders put five to six hundred miles on their bikes is not only for physical benefits; it is also to give the rider the advantage of learning the full operation of his bike.

The efficient rider travels smoothly, unwaveringly, and effortlessly — not exactly the description of the typical Wandering Wheels rider the first few days on his bike. He not only uses the muscles of his thighs, but also those of his lower legs, the feet, the arms, the back, and the abdomen. The more muscles used, the less work each muscle has to do, and the longer each can work without tiring.

By bending the foot down on the bottom of his stroke, the rider can pedal considerably past bottom center. Then by rapidly bending the foot forward, he can press his pedal over top center. In this manner, the rider can provide an even pressure around the entire stroke. Less force is then needed and the bike is propelled more smoothly and with less wobbling.

This method of pedaling, called ankling, is the trademark of any good cyclist. The method is especially helpful in hillclimbing. The Wandering Wheels rider is advised to start practicing ankling at once. If practiced at slow speeds on hills (like the little rises in Indiana), it can be learned in time for the great mountain ranges of the West.

Practice in riding in a straight line at high speeds is also encouraged. The ability to ride in a line, not wavering more than three or four inches at high speeds or up a hill, is important as a safety factor. Riding straight keeps the cyclist within a few inches of the road's edge and out of the path of motorists.

When riding into the wind, the novice rider learns to reduce his gear to keep the normal pedal speed. By reducing the gear, the rider reduces his forward speed, but retains his pedal speed with no extra effort. The same is true of hillclimbing. The rider reduces his gear until he reaches a comfortable pace, not worrying about the speed with which he mounts the summit.

A final preparation for the tour is packing for the trip. Depending upon the length of their trips, the number of items differ. The Wandering Wheels rider, however, will need these basics: socks, shorts, riding jerseys or knitted sport shirts or the equivalent, a long-sleeve light sweater or sweat shirt, a light nylon jacket, rain gear, a hat for protection from the sun and rain (but with a small bill so as not to build up extra wind resistance), gloves, tennis shoes or cycling shoes.

With bike, sleeping bag and tent provided for the Wandering Wheels rider, the novice is ready to begin his tour. Hopefully, the preparation will be adequate. Despite the preliminaries, however, those first few days and weeks can be torturous, as expressed by this Wandering Wheels alumnus: "The first day out, I seriously doubted my sanity and wondered whatever possessed me to undertake such a venture. I was undoubtedly more tired, pained, and miserable than I had ever been in my life.

"I found it easy to complain and to hate. I just couldn't see any sense in feeling so miserable.

"After I fell off my bike, I had my doubts as to whether I would ever ride again. When Coach came over to help me up and said, 'Next time point your toes,' I knew I had to get on that bike again."

11

"It's downhill all the way."

A typical day for the Wandering Wheels rider begins about two weeks out on the tour. By then he's pretty well oriented; he knows what he can expect on the trip the next day. He's a well-oiled machine, so to speak, and he's a little bit cocky and self-sufficient.

Two weeks out would put the riders approximately in eastern Colorado. At this point the land is mostly uncluttered, but the rider has been pretty well awe-stricken by what the West has had to offer. He's seen the beauty of God's country as he never has before — at about fifteen miles per hour.

The worst part of any day — and especially if you have ridden 120 miles the day before — is getting up in the morning. The Wheels have gone to bed about ten o'clock the night before, and now, at five in the morning, it's time to get up. It's been a Wandering Wheels tradition that a rider doesn't wake up as normally as he would back home.

"No nudge by mom; no dad calling from downstairs; no alarm clock ringing; or no clock radio gently blaring out good-morning music," says Davenport. None of these work on a Wandering Wheels tour.

"You walk into a room where there are about forty guys sleeping in their sheetliners on top of their sleeping bags all over the floor," describes Davenport. "They look like a pack of ghosts

"He's seen the beauty of God's country as he never has before. . . ."

lined along the floor, some of them tucked away with their pillows placed over their heads to keep away the morning rays.

"Now if you were to walk in there and say, 'Time to rise and shine,' you'd be lucky if they heard you. If you walked in and played music or rang off an alarm clock, you might get a few guys to roll over into a more comfortable position. No, no standard techniques have worked in earlier Wandering Wheels trips, so we devised some of our own."

Through the years Davenport has learned that the trick is to jolt the riders out of the sack. For example, if they are sleeping in a gymnasium, the Wandering Wheels leaders always make sure there are a couple of basketballs left out the night before. Then when it's time for the riders to rise, one of the leaders will walk around dribbling the ball around the heads of the slumbering ghosts. "It's impossible to continue to sleep with this going on," says Davenport. "But we still get a few who try for a few extra winks. When this happens, those who are up begin throwing the ball back and forth, and — *oops!* — they toss short, landing the ball on top of one of the sleeping beauties."

Another method the Wandering Wheels have used can be employed where there is access to some kind of amplification — such as turning on a church organ and pulling out all the stops on the bass pedal.

"One place we slept in had a couple of cymbals. Man, when we banged those together, those guys came screaming out of their sacks like the whole world was coming apart!" Davenport found he could get a similar effect by banging an old pot with a big spoon. "Usually, dropping a large number of metal folding chairs on a concrete floor rattles them enough to have them do what you ask."

When nothing else works, Davenport resorts to the water treatment. This is a standard, fail-safe, camp system. Davenport and the other riders take the water bottles off their handlebars and proceed to squirt them at first. If the sleeper doesn't move fast enough, the guys remove the bottle caps and dump the remaining water on him. This not only bolts them out of the bag, but means that their sleeping gear is going to be a little damp the following night.

"We can't even say, 'Chow's on' — that doesn't work. You've

got to employ something as loud as a cannon and something tough enough to get them crawling up a wall."

The first thing the Wandering Wheels do out of the sack is to check the wind. Even before they roll up their bag, they're runing outside to see which way the flags on the bikes are blowing. If they're blowing the right direction — a tail wind — the riders are set for the day. Unhappily, most of the mornings the wind seems to be blowing against them.

The riders return to their sleeping bags and roll them up so they aren't tempted to crawl back in. Then they take care of their personal needs — going to the toilet, washing, showering if they can, combing their hair, and shaving. Then they patiently wait around for breakfast.

When the cook calls, "Chow's on," the guys scramble for the food. Generally they eat pancakes, cereal, Tang, and cocoa — that's about it. And whether the cereal is oatmeal or some brand of dry cereal, the riders get into little skirmishes about the proper way to serve it.

The fight over the oatmeal centers around one thing: raisins. "Some of our fellas like raisins in the oatmeal and several don't," explains Davenport. "So it's a constant battle. They just can't have them hard in the oatmeal, they've got to have them boiled in, so they're nice and soft."

The argument over the cold cereal centers on whether you should put on the sugar first and then the milk, or whether you should pour on the milk first. "We've found on each trip that the kids are divided about fifty-fifty on both sides," says Davenport.

Each guy will put away about five or six pancakes. Sometimes the cook will doctor them up with a fruit supplement such as blueberries. On days the leaders feel a little "plush," they will add some bacon or sausage or hamburger to the breakfast menu.

After breakfast there are several tasks the riders must perform to get their bikes ready for the day's ride. First, they check their tires for proper air pressure, and if they find a flat, they fix it. The bicycles should be kept clean and dry; only a few minutes are required to wipe off the dew and the dust and the road grease.

The chain and derailleur are cleaned relatively easily. All the parts are exposed. Wiping off the oil and dirt with a clean cloth is all that is necessary. Occasionally, the chain should be lubricated, so from time to time the riders will turn their bike upside down and slowly rotate the crank while oiling each link.

The riders also check the equipment's various nuts and bolts and screws, particularly after a rough ride the day before, and tighten those that need it. Brake and gear cables are also checked for wear and breakage.

While others are finishing up their maintenance check, some are putting on their Chap-Stick and zinc oxide to protect their lips and nose and other exposed areas from the sun. They have the appearance of warriors preparing for battle.

With the fellows up, their personal needs cared for, their gear stowed in the trailer, their breakfast in their stomachs and all the arguments, pro and con, on the relative merits of raisins or non-raisins in the oatmeal, their bodies and equipment in shape for the day's ride, Davenport brings the group together for a time of reflection. "Devotions play a relevant role in the Wandering Wheels program," Davenport explains. "In the past we've studied the life of Jesus as recorded in the Gospels and the lives of the early Christians as recorded in the Book of Acts.

"We take about twenty minutes to study together, sing a song or two, pray, then break up into smaller groups of five or six to talk and share the merits of the morning's study. Over the years we've had comments from the fellas to the effect that this time is what really ties the group and the program together."

Normally after this time of reflection, the riders do any last-minute checking or chores they must do before time to head out. The entire group is divided into four or five teams that ride about five minutes apart for safety purposes. When it's time to go, Davenport yells, "First group out!" and the first six or seven riders head down the road.

The first stop of the morning can be anywhere from ten to thirty-five miles ahead, depending upon the wind. Usually it's about fifteen miles. Davenport systematically calls out, "Second group out!" then "Third group out!" etc., until all the groups are pedaling down the highway about a mile apart. "There's little talking on the first leg," he says. "Most of the guys are just thinking about what kind of day is ahead of them and concentrating on what they are doing."

At the end of the first leg the riders will stop at a filling station or little store and buy some gum or some coffee and a roll. After that, they're ready to wing down the highway; they'll push for another ten or fifteen miles in good style.

"They'll try to get 50 or 60 or more miles behind them in the morning," says Davenport. "Normally, they'll put on more miles in the morning than in the afternoon. It's a psychological factor with them more than anything else. If they're pushing for 120 miles that day, they'll want to get at least 60 miles behind them before lunch."

As they make their way down the highway in the morning, the riders are going to stop two or three times, and they are going to meet a variety of people. If they are near some town at about 10:30 in the morning, usually some local newspaper will have a reporter come out with a photographer for a story. "The guys like the publicity," says their leader, "but they're anxious to keep moving to get those miles behind them. Secretly they appreciate the attention and psychologically it's good for their egos, particularly when they see the story in the paper, but it does tend to hold them back. Sometimes some of the fellas will stay behind for an interview, and the others will ride ahead after the pictures are taken."

For lunchtime, the Wandering Wheels scout tries to find the best facility where the riders can take advantage of the toilets. If the plumbing isn't good, thirty-five to forty guys can play havoc with a toilet system. Out West, where the towns are few and far between, toilets are hard to find. Having the truck and trailer provides the group with some privacy.

When a rider had to urinate, he'd "whiz" — as the Wheels came to term it — against one of the tires on the shoulder side of the vehicles. The roadside tire at the rear of the truck traditionally became associated with that type of activity. Davenport estimates that the tire took on about three or four gallons of urine a day.

One of the riders bought a "Gentlemen" sign and attached it to the truck above the wheel. But the experience that capped off the entire 1968 trip happened after the tire went flat. "The guy who took off the tire we'd been whizzing on all summer couldn't understand why we were all doubled up with laughter. When he got it off, he couldn't find what was wrong with it. Of course we knew it had died of exhaustion."

Working with forty young men who have to use the john can be time consuming. Often the station proprietors will encourage them to use both of the rooms — the men's and the women's. On the Wheels 1969 trip from Miami to Seattle, the riders rolled into a town about fifty miles north of Denver, and decided to camp at a roadside park which had two johns. All evening the fellas had been taking advantage of using the extra facility. There hadn't been much traffic that evening, and the fellas felt quite free to use both. There would be ample time to warn someone if the facility was occupied.

As one of the Wheels was using the women's john, casually taking his time, suddenly a car whipped up and a young woman stepped out. "She was obviously in need of the facility," Davenport recalls, "and she hurriedly ran toward the john. We were too far away to warn her, and she had moved inside too quickly to stop her.

"The guy inside, the most innocent guy you'd ever meet, suddenly heard these footsteps of a woman rapidly approaching the door. She opened the door and stepped inside. Our guy, sitting on the toilet in one of the stalls, froze. There he was, with his big, black canvas tennis shoes and hairy legs. He quickly tucked his feet up onto the stool, so he couldn't be seen under the partition, and sweat blood. He stayed in that position until whoever it was finished her business and left."

The guys outside could hardly contain their laughter when the woman walked out. It was like they were sitting on a timebomb. Then, a few moments later when this guy stepped out of the john, as embarrassed as he could be, the group exploded.

Taking care of personal needs rarely gets much attention once the fellows have relieved themselves. At lunch they try to park the truck and trailer near a little restaurant or store where the riders can supplement their meal with some extras.

A typical lunch would include two bologna sandwiches, lettuce, maybe a peanut butter and jelly sandwich, potato chips or corn curls, Kool Aid and some heavy cookies. Sometimes the cook will bring out some soup, but when they're hot, the riders don't care for it.

". . . a half-hour to rest. . . ."

Normally, when they have finished eating they hope Davenport will tell them they have about a half-hour to rest. Most of them will find a place to sack out, spreading out on the grass and dozing until the first call: "First group out!" As they pedal down the road for the first leg of the afternoon, the staff remains behind to clean up the equipment and to get things ready for the next rendezvous. Then the truck moves down the highway ahead of the riders who look forward to meeting it down the road.

The afternoon drags a little. After they are back on their bikes, after working hard all morning, the Wheels know they still have at least fifty miles ahead of them. Each pack tries to space out its day well enough so the riders don't find themselves pushing harder than necessary. The guys might ride hard during a certain leg of the trip, however, so they can spend more time in a town with a particular attraction.

Of course, one of the biggest attractions is people. An important part of the Wandering Wheels' day occurs when they find someone interested in filling them in on a little local history. When it comes to giving directions, however, the fellows have come to the conclusion that no one knows distances or how many hills there are in the area. "Unless you've ridden a bike recently," says Davenport, "you don't know what a hill is. A 1 percent grade on a bike is a hill. When you're in a car, you don't notice it until a hill reaches about 8 percent grade. It wasn't long before our fellas learned not to ask such questions."

On one trip a group of riders met an old man in Kansas and asked him how far it was to the next town. He said it was about five miles. "Are there any hills," a rider asked. "It's downhill all

". . . one of the biggest attractions is people."

the way," the old man replied. But the riders later learned that the town was twice the distance away, and there were several "up-hills" along the way.

"We tell our riders to just ride, and don't trust anyone else's judgment. Just use your common sense, and trust God to pull you through the difficult places," Davenport advises.

The remainder of the afternoon is spent meeting with the truck, taking care of flat tires on the bikes, or putting more zinc oxide on the exposed areas and, salve on cuts and bruises. Everyone is kept busy.

The cooks are moving in and out of stores along the way, looking for special bargains and looking for special treats that will make the evening meal a little different. About 5:30 or 6 o'clock the riders have their objective in view, and they start to get excited about where they will spend the night and whether or not they will have showers.

About 50 percent of the time they will stay in a church. About 25 percent of the time they will stay in an armory or other civic building. The remaining 25 percent of the time they will camp out in a ball park or under a pavilion, or in someone's back yard.

The first group into town locates the truck and trailer which has gone ahead to make all the arrangements. After the first pack rolls in, the pots and pans are broken out to prepare for supper. The first question the riders ask is, "Can we get to some showers?" There is nothing better than a warm shower to get all the salt off their bodies, they say.

If they get to swim, that really tops off the day. Perhaps the community's near a lake or it has a community pool or someone in the town has a private pool and opens it up to the guys.

The next questions the riders ask is, "What are the ground rules?" and "Do we have a meeting tonight?" Normally, the Wandering Wheels will hold a concert in the small town, most often in a church or in a park. It comes as a little extra hard work after a hard day, but the fellows speak of their meetings as some of the most meaningful experiences of their trip. The warm responses of the people give them both a psychological and a spiritual lift.

While some of the fellows are helping prepare the dinner, others are off at the local laundromat to do their laundry. Still others are repairing their bikes, and a few are sacking out.

After the evening program the fellows are free to do what they want. Usually there are some young people who want to talk with them more about the trip. Often they are taken to a home for ice cream. An older guy may corner some girl who ends up doing his laundry for him.

Yet there is one fact about the Wandering Wheels that never changes: Davenport never has to worry about getting his riders to bed. There's no fooling around; once they hit the sack, they're down for good. Before they know it, another day is with them.

". . . a concert in a small town. . . ."

12

"... like a bunch of piglets...."

As mentioned previously, meals on the trail follow a general pattern of cereal for breakfast; sandwiches, potato chips, and fruit for lunch; and stew or hamburgers for supper. "When the body's been working as hard as theirs," Coach Davenport explains, "they're so hungry they'll eat anything. I've seen them eat four-day-old donuts and stale bread. In Wyoming where filling stations and stores are seventy-five miles apart, they have little choice other than to just brush off the mold.

"Most of these kids come from middle class homes and at home would gripe if the eggs were a bit runny. But on the trail, they doctor up their powdered milk with honey, cocoa, sugar, or anything else they can find to make a little variety."

Surprisingly, despite the fact that athletics is seriously practiced by so many people, there is little information about the diets and food preferences of athletes. Most of the books on coaching and practically all the journals devoted to sports do not mention diet. When the topic is alluded to, the only statement that appears is that a wholesome, varied diet should be consumed.

One outstanding characteristic of training tables is the large amount of protein served. Such practice is based on a variety of psychological factors rather than physiological requirements, however. When on its 1966 cross-country trip, the Wandering Wheels stopped in the home of one of the riders in Fairborn, Ohio, and demolished sixty-two pounds of meat in one meal and took thirty pounds of meat along for sandwiches later in the day, this wasn't because they needed the protein. Meat had been scarce on that trip, but the real benefit of the meal was its psychological effect on the riders. For years, evidence has been conclusive that athletes require no more dietary protein, even during strenuous training, than other individuals. Any ordinary diet provides sufficient extra protein to build additional muscle tissue.

"We in no way consider ourselves authorities on the best kinds of foods to eat or not to eat," Davenport admits. "We just try to feed the riders a balanced diet on about a dollar each per day.

"Of course we're counting on some people like that family in Ohio, to give us a helping hand. Once a week we get a carry-out dinner that really hits the spot. Then twice each week we find that somebody will provide us with enough money to eat in a restaurant. We don't generally eat better in a restaurant, but it's a treat for the riders to eat with silverware, tablecloths, and sparkling water glasses."

Sometimes the cooks like to experiment. On the first cross-country trip, a cook cranked out some sloppy-joes for a stop at Rock River, Wyoming, that literally had the fellows holding a water glass in one hand and the food in the other. The sauce was so hot that they had to take a gulp of water with every bite.

On the same trip in Reno, Nevada, the cyclists met a bicycle nut who shared an energy-food idea which didn't take much preparation. He called the concoction "gorp," and it was made of equal portions of raisins, M&M candies, and peanuts. "It contained all the basic ingredients you needed for quick energy. You buy big sacks of each and mix them together. It was quite tasty."

There are two nutrients that are required in increased amounts by those engaged in vigorous physical activity such as cycling. The most important of these is water. The other is salt. For most riders, the requirement for salt, even during periods of excessive perspiration, can be met by extra seasoning of the food.

Traditionally, water has been restricted for those engaged in heavy physical activity. But today there is considerable practical evidence that consuming water during such activity can be beneficial. The importance of maintaining the water balance during athletic competition stems from the fact that the primary accompaniment of dehydration is fatigue.

On one of their cross-country trips, the Wandering Wheels came to the Kansas-Colorado border desperate for water. They spotted a stainless steel irrigation setup stretching out for miles across a wheat field. The riders jumped off their bikes and grabbed the spigots and drank to their hearts' content. "From a distance," says Davenport, "they looked like a bunch of piglets getting nourishment from Mamma pig."

But perhaps the liquid they drink the most comes free off the truck — Kool-Aid. There would be no way to estimate just how much of that drink, which they nicknamed, "cyclamate," they have consumed over the years.

Anytime the riders are in Florida they like to steer to places where they advertise, "All you can drink [orange juice] — 10¢." When the proprietors see the Wheels coming, they wish they were closed. In fact, in one place the manager gave the fellows just one glass, and told them that's all they could drink for a dime. Another proprietor told the fellows that they shouldn't drink more than two glasses, because it wouldn't be good for them.

"We ran into a health nut on one of our trips," recalls Davenport, "who was against our fellas taking in any hard sugar. He advocated we take in the natural sugars by drinking juices. But we found that nothing else quenches the thirst better than a carbonated drink."

Davenport has estimated that on two of their crossings, the Wandering Wheels have drunk as many as ten thousand bottles of pop per trip. One rider on the thousand-mile trip, Dan Reedy, still holds the record for downing twenty-one carbonated drinks in one day — and most of those were sixteen-ounce bottles. At one stop alone he drank sixty-four ounces.

"Our fellas think the A&W Root Beer stands are the best places to quench their thirst," Davenport says. "One reason is that they can buy a whole quart at one time. The root beer comes in a cone-shaped, wax carton, and our fellas have completely wiped out their supply at some stands.

"They've even been set up a few times. One owner in eastern Colorado saw the first group of six come in and told them the drinks were on the house. He didn't realize there were thirty-four other thirsty guys just behind, but he graciously set up the entire group.

"Our guys were out in the street waving in our fellas for this special treat."

The riders are always looking for the best bargain for their money, of course. Occasionally, they'll find a place that still sells pop for ten cents a bottle. The fellas take full advantage of the supply. But they've been taken advantage of, too. One day on the '68 tour, the Wheels had to get off their bikes and walk over a construction area. When they came to the top of a hill, they saw a man selling pop. But he was selling it for thirty-five cents a can! "It was proverbial highway robbery," says Davenport, "Our guys were really thirsty, but they were too smart to let this man cheat them. They went without the drink."

Davenport has seen a pop machine beaten on, stomped on, kicked, and every other violence imaginable done to it when it hasn't delivered the goods. The riders find nothing more exasperating than to ride up to a lone pop machine, drop a coin into the slot, and get nothing in return. There have been times that it didn't even return the money. More important to them, they didn't get their drink.

On one trip Davenport took a ten-gallon thermo-type cooler. The guys would take the lid off and dump a chunk of ice inside and fill it with juice. Davenport drilled a hole in the truck bed and ran a nylon line through the opening into the back of the truck where they had placed the jug. The jug was situated at such a height that when the hose was lowered, the juice flowed out naturally. This way each rider could fill his cup with little trouble.

"Of course, we found after a few days that the guys just put their mouths over it and sucked out the juice," says Davenport. "But we put a stop to that, warning them of K.P. if they were caught. And every once in a while, I'd come around the truck and find one of the guys sucking on the tube."

Davenport found that the groups that have ridden with the Wandering Wheels have been able to protect themselves from any serious sickness by washing their personal mess kits individually — never in a common pot. Only once have the Wheels encountered any serious illness. On their 1968 trip they had stopped at the Grand Canyon to have what they called "a thousand-mile ceremony." Everyone took from their lockers some snacks and

100

threw them in a pot. There was candy, cookies, pretzels, gum — every type of snack imaginable. They also made a special drink of lemonade. It was tasty, but not everyone got a drink of it. Good thing. An hour later, everyone who had tasted of the lemonade was throwing up. It was an uncomfortable night.

Actually, when you evaluate some of the eating habits of the Wandering Wheels, you find that they leave much to be desired. Of the entire program, this aspect could be improved. The riders too often gulp down some weird concoctions and eat nutritionless products, the money for which might be spent better in the long run.

One favorite treat the riders enjoy is to take a bag of peanuts and dump them into a carbonated drink. There's no doubt about it to the thirsty riders: it's refreshing to slurp down a few peanuts now and then as you drink your pop. But it offers very little food value. Like eating extra amounts of protein, it has a valuable psychological effect — as do the Snicker bars, Look bars, licorice, marshmallow peanuts, and Tootsie Pops they consume.

"In every group," explains Davenport, "you'll have a guy with some kind of fetish. One guy, I remember, couldn't get enough Tootsie Pops. He'd go into a store and buy out its supply. Another guy's kick was salt water taffy. And there was another who always had a stick of Juicy Fruit gum."

Of course there were always the cookies from home. By the time they would reach the Wandering Wheels on the trail, they would be broken to bits. But they'd enjoy the crumbs, anyway. And they enjoyed the dry brownies from home, too.

A favorite meal over the years with the Wandering Wheels has been the fruit plate. The base is a section of watermelon. To this they would add a number ten can of fruit cocktail, a number ten can of peaches, some bananas, grapes, and apples. Sometimes they'd throw in some raisins and prunes. Before serving, the dish would be chilled in ice. "We serve this specialty once a week," Davenport remarks. "It really loosens up the guys."

Pizza is a favorite, too. Though the Wheels aren't served the treat, they have opportunity to get it in town once a week. Spaghetti is big. So is hamburger. "We'll serve each rider a half to three-quarters of a pound of meat with a pile of potatoes," says Davenport. "And gravy — they love gravy."

Generally, the cooks try to keep away from the greasy foods. They try to give the riders all the meat they can in sloppy-joes. They serve ham once a week. Stewing beef, carrots, celery, and cabbage is put in a pot and cooked a couple of hours to let the juices work through. Lots of bread and butter.

The hardest meal to prepare is lunch. After a couple of weeks the riders tire of peanut butter and jelly sandwiches. The cooks will sometimes come up with a tuna casserole, which they boiled up in the morning and let cool off. The riders use it as sandwich spread.

Toasted cheese sandwiches are well accepted, particularly on a cold day, when served with tomato soup.

One of the greatest treats the Wheels have on a trip is to be told one afternoon that at the end of their ride, they are going to eat at a smorgasbord house. This has become a regular experience in Salt Lake City, Utah. The cost is only $1.25 a person. Wandering Wheels pays the dollar, and the riders each chip in the 25¢. Needless to say, they always do justice to the meal.

Another regular trip stop is at Robbies Restaurant in Topeka, Kansas. Here you can eat all the chicken you want for a couple of dollars. At one stop, the riders stayed for an hour and a half. Before they left the restaurant, they had stuffed away seventy chickens.

When you're one of the Wandering Wheels, you get hungry.

"When you're one of the Wandering Wheels, you get hungry."

102

13

"... don't worry about Ken."

On their second trip of 1967, the Wandering Wheels were moving along as normally as could be expected for a large group of high school riders. There were several fourteen-year-olds on the trip, and to be honest about it, the younger riders kept Davenport on edge most of the way. In fact, this was the trip after which he seriously questioned whether he should continue with the program for safety's sake, or quit while he was ahead.

It seems the younger the riders are, the less seriously they observe safety precautions. Perhaps it is because the younger are more naive; it's difficult to know the reasons. All Davenport knew was that the younger riders often did foolish things on their bikes, much to the irritation of the older riders and to the anxiety of the leaders. To counter some of their antics, Davenport cracked an ornery whip.

Moving across Wyoming one morning along Interstate 70 (what used to be U.S. Route 40), Davenport waited for the last group of riders to pull out, then pulled ahead on his motorcycle to check on how they were doing. The last groups checked out well, and he rumbled ahead to catch up to the first group out that morning.

As he was wheeling along, he saw ahead of him a flashing red light. Cars were pulled alongside the highway, and as he got closer Davenport could see that there had been a wreck involving at least two cars — a serious accident.

"My heart went right down to the toenail of my big toe," Davenport recalls. "I feared that we had had our first wreck."

But as he drew closer to the scene, Davenport spotted one of his riders directing traffic, and the fellow yelled, "No fear, Coach, none of our guys was involved."

Davenport parked his motorcycle and walked over to the spot where two cars had collided. A drunk driving an old Plymouth had gotten on the Interstate some forty miles up the road on the wrong side. The police had been trying to stop him and to control traffic down the superhighway, but before anything could be done, the man slammed head-on into an Oldsmobile from Oregon.

The Plymouth was totally wiped out in the median strip. The drunk lay outside the battered machine, very much dead. The other car, too, was totaled, but the family inside had not been seriously injured.

One of the young riders, Larry Dillon, who was a senior in high school at the time, had tried to minister to the dying man's needs. Larry was one of the more serious riders on the trip, and had a deep interest in medicine. "The guys told me that Larry had approached that dying man with his vile breath hanging about him and a yellow mucous oozing from his mouth, and had tried to give him mouth-to-mouth resuscitation. When I heard that, I could hardly believe it. The thought of it turned my stomach.

"Later on down the highway, I spotted Larry throwing up alongside the road. The whole experience had finally caught up to him, and his body was beginning to react. He threw up all day long, until the shock wore off."

That incident left a serious note in the group. Even more, it was an unusual life-changing experience for a boy out there on the highway. The experience riveted Larry's ambition and purpose to his heart. He finished his last year in pre-med at Taylor in 1970.

For the other riders, the incident made them feel a little closer to God having seen a life slip away before their eyes on the highway.

Davenport believes that part of the significance of the Wandering Wheels program is that there's enough of the element of danger in it that the riders are constantly living on the edge of life, knowing that God is constantly undergirding them.

106

Discipline and order are as necessary to the expeditions as any other part of the program. The fellows ride in packs of four or five with a veteran Wheel leading the pack. They start at regular well-spaced intervals. The bright flags flying from their antennas warn motorists that there is something ahead just over the knoll. On straight-a-ways the bright orange of the flag and back patch is visible for miles.

The value of these safety devices is incalculable. When vehicles are travelling at speeds in excess of sixty or seventy miles

"They start at regular well-spaced intervals."

per hour, the driver is upon a bicycle rider before he even sees him, unless he is warned in advance.

On two-lane highways where there are no shoulders and there is heavy traffic, the riders pedal single-file. But they don't like riding that way; it's boring, and they can't carry on a conversation while pedaling down the road. On broader highways with adequate shoulders, therefore, the riders push along two abreast.

In each pack the fellows ride with about four or five yards between them and the riders ahead. A novice cyclist tends to overlap a tire with the rider in front. Sixty percent of the Wheels' spills are a result of such crowding. If the rider aheads stops or runs over a twig or needs to avoid a slick spot or pothole in the road, he needs room to maneuver. If tires overlap, they bump, and there's a spill.

Sometimes the riders will fudge on this rule, particularly when there's a strong head wind. The riders behind like to crowd up as closely as possible to the cyclist ahead to take advantage of the wind break. But Davenport keeps reminding them of the safety factor, and if that doesn't work, a few scrapes and bruises from the pavement serve as a reminder.

On the back roads with little traffic, some of the safety rules can be relaxed. The riders will bunch up in such instances and get into a heated debate. Or when they are riding along on a closed section of highway, like an interstate extension not yet open to motor vehicles, they can prank around a little in order to break the monotony.

Davenport has never encouraged night riding, and only on a few occasions has it been necessary. The bikes are equipped with battery-operated flasher lights to warn approaching motorists, in the event they do travel after dark. Riding directly into the sun in late afternoon is also taboo on a Wandering Wheels tour. Anytime a driver cannot see 100 percent, the riders know that they are riding with a real handicap.

The higher speeds obtained with the lightweight bike, coupled with the thin tire, require more careful attention to the road than under normal circumstances. The riders are told to get into the habit of glancing far enough ahead to mentally take notes of the road's defects, of its side roads and cross traffic, of its stops. Also, the riders need to watch for oil slicks or gravel patches, which

"Discipline and order. . . ."

could easily throw them off balance. Cattle stops imbedded in back roads or car tracks or railroad track crossings also need to be approached cautiously. Large stones, sticks, potholes, or breaks in the pavement should be avoided not only for safety's sake, but for the sake of the bicycle and tires.

Gravel or slippery spots on corners can be extremely dangerous if not approached properly. Wandering Wheels are warned to grasp the handle bars tightly in such instances, with the arms straight and tense. Never lean, turn, or brake on such a spot.

The Wandering Wheels' most serious wrecks have been in the mountains. The Wheel who holds the record so far for being most seriously injured rode on the Wandering Wheels 1968 cross-country tour. This is the trip that was filmed by travelogue producer Julian Gromer. The aftermath of the accident is part of the documentary of the trip.

Ken Bell, the rider, had been leaning over his bike for a long time during the coast down the Sierra Nevadas into Bishop, California. As is the proper custom, he had positioned his body over the length of the bicycle to create less wind resistance. Near the end of the coast, after his bike had slowed down to about thirty-five miles per hour, he sat up on his saddle to relax.

His body's response was similar to what happens when you've been squatting and suddenly stand up — the blood rushes into areas that before had been closed off, leaving your head, and you feel faint. So Kenny fainted, and of course he lost control of his bike.

He fell off, hitting the abrasive asphalt at the same speed as his bike. It had been a hot day, and the only clothes he had on to protect him were his riding shorts. His body was skinned up badly. "His right shoulder was torn down to the muscle, and his knees and waist were all torn up," says Davenport. "He was pretty badly beaten. He was in the hospital for five days. It took the doctors several hours to pick out the gravel."

Just after Ken had been injured and was still lying along the road, along came a relative of Roy Flannery, one of the other riders. He had been looking for Roy, knowing that the Wheels were passing through his area.

He helped get Ken into the convertible, from which the filming was being done, and off to the hospital. He was so impressed

110

with the group and what they were trying to accomplish he told Davenport to continue with the tour, and he would take care of Ken. "I'll be his 'guardian,'" he said. "You go on ahead and don't worry about Ken. When he's well enough to be released from the hospital, I'll fly him to wherever you are."

Five days later Ken was out of the hospital. The man chartered a plane and flew him to Las Vegas, Nevada. There, he put Ken on a bus to be driven to Kingman, Arizona, where the Wheels had ridden ahead.

"His arms were still pink when he joined us," Davenport recalls, "but Ken finished the trip with us. It is this kind of involvement by people we hardly knew that has given us the confidence that God is watching over us and telling us to keep hanging in there."

14

"Boy, was I tight!"

On the initial Wandering Wheels trip in 1964, on the very first day before the riders had reached the first town of their thousand-mile journey, they spotted a water tower and estimated that the town was just ahead. It wasn't. They kept pedaling and pedaling, and that water tower seemed to keep moving and moving ahead of them, never any closer.

That kind of discouragement is bad enough. Add to it the local native's "knowledge" of distances between points, and it's worse. But perhaps the most cruel of all are the advertising signs that play on the rider's mind that there's a stop just ahead.

Out in the desert areas in particular, when you near a town, you begin to see such signs advertising places to eat. The closer you get, the more signs you see. The Wandering Wheels saw countless such signs between the two coasts which border the United States. They would be riding along, tired, thirsty, perspiration soaking their bodies, and suddenly would come upon a sign that said ten miles to such and such a place.

Immediately their saliva glands would begin to function, if there was enough moisture in them. The adrenalin begins to flow within their bodies, and they pump a little harder and faster to make that last ten miles. And then they come around a corner and spot the state highway sign marking the distance to the town: fifteen more miles, not ten! Suddenly they realize that once again they've been duped by some advertiser who's after their business.

What's a few extra miles in a car? the ad men probably reason. But on a bike, it's murder. One of the Wandering Wheels would scream at the top of his lungs when he saw one of these contradictions. He vowed to make a law making such advertising illegal, and would come back some day and sue everyone of those people for lying to him.

There have been other times that the riders have had to kneel under unexpected blows when they've reached a town. On the salt flats in Utah during one trip, the Wheels had ridden for miles without a break, seeing nothing but the chalky flats moving slowly beneath their tires. Finally they reached a little store, tired, worn mentally and physically from having to fight with the traffic and being exposed to the elements.

Spotting a road sign miles back made them anticipate a satisfying stop at a gas station and roadside store. But when they got inside, they discovered that the National Guard had been there just the day before and had cleaned out the place. All the pop and candy were gone. All the ice cream was gone. There was only some stale popcorn. The guys were bluer when they left the place than when they had arrived.

"So often I've felt that kids — particularly the churched kids — are like hot house plants," says Davenport. "They've never had a hard experience. The discouragement they must face on a Wandering Wheels tour is the best thing that could happen to them. It's great for their spiritual growth.

"To grow up, a person needs to court danger and discouragement in order to watch God take him through it. Our riders have had the highest spiritual experiences of their lives on these trips. There have been times when mountain climbing has left them with no strength, but when brought to this point, the riders have come to acknowledge that they can't make it on their own; they must rely on God for His help. As a result, they learn to depend on Him."

One night the Wheels pulled into town dead tired and were told that the camp site they were to stay in was at the other end of town — five miles away. That just about wiped them out. When they got to camp, they took showers, ate, and climbed into their sleeping bags and fell asleep. They were tired; they were discouraged. Worse, they were literally beaten by circumstances.

114

But after the night's rest, they woke up to a new, bright morning. It was like a new beginning.

"It is usually sweet bliss, just to settle down at night knowing that all that is behind you has given you the right to sleep for several hours — that you don't have to go any further that day. There's consolation in that," says Davenport. "It gets to the place that you hate that miserable piece of metal that has become your taskmaster."

Davenport recalls riding over a bridge on one of the trips and spotting one of the Wandering Wheels resting alongside the road with his head in his hands. He was a football player on the Taylor team — the team center and linebacker. "John [Tindale] didn't say to me, 'Hey, wait for me.' No, he was whipped. He just said, 'I'll see ya down the road.'

"The bike really teaches a guy how to swallow pride — how to admit that you're whipped. You soon learn how vulnerable you are. You learn to trust God and to apply Christian principles to the negatives."

The Wandering Wheels have spent enough days on the road to know from experience that the negatives don't just pile up on the discouraging days. They also have a way of breaking in on the "good" days. Joe Prillwitz, a rider on the Wheels 1969 Miami to Seattle trip can testify to that. He and a troupe of other riders had been making good time between Trapville, Alabama, and Columbus, Mississippi.

As they approached Tuscaloosa, they had a good tailwind and were really burning off the miles. They rode ahead of the other packs, and anxious to get to Columbus, the first mail stop of the trip, they took only fifteen minutes for lunch and pushed ahead.

Near Tuscaloosa, Joe and the other riders with him spotted a man on the side of the road, and when they neared him, he waved them down.

"Where you guys headed?" he asked.

"Columbus, Mississippi, today," Joe answered. "Eventually to Seattle."

The man seemed interested and had a number of questions, but Joe and his group wanted to get going, so they suggested the man talk to their leader.

"A guy named Davenport should be along here soon on a motorcycle," they told the man. "He can tell you all about the trip." And with that they pedaled away.

The afternoon was hot, and just outside of Tuscaloosa the small pack of riders ran into some hills. Worn, but still high with anticipation of nearing their destination, the riders decided to stop for a rest at a gas station. Joe tells what happened next: "The thermometer inside the station said it was 106 degrees. We figured maybe we'd better slow down until Coach could catch up to us and tell us just how far we had to go.

"The best we could figure it, we still had forty miles, and it was about 3:30 in the afternoon. We didn't want to get too far ahead and then have to double back.

"Pretty soon Coach roared up on his motorcycle, and we asked how far back the other guys were. He said they were back in Tuscaloosa waiting for us to come back.

"Boy, was I tight! Here, we found out that this man had talked to Davenport and convinced him to stay in town that night for a free meal and for a concert. That was twenty miles back."

As it turned out, Davenport took pity on the riders and told them to wait at the gas station; he would send the truck to pick them up. That night the riders had a free meal and a comfortable place to stay. They sang over the University of Alabama radio station — and in a women's dormitory!

"We had T-bone steak," Joe remembers, "And that sing in the girl's dorm wasn't hard to take, so I guess it all worked out all right. At first I was pretty discouraged about the whole incident, but the Lord seemed to work it out just right."

15

"The single most discouraging part of any Wandering Wheels trip is the wind," says Davenport. "You can conquer a hill, spit on it, throw rocks at it; you can get mad at the trucks and tell off the driver if you meet him down the road; but the wind you can't buck.

"We've had guys literally blown off their bikes. We've had them stopped in their tracks when trucks have whizzed past. When you're riding against a twenty-mile-an-hour wind, the suction from a truck can stop you dead."

Benny Lester, a Wandering Wheels rider, would holler and scream and call the wind all kinds of names. He was always looking for ways he could "hurt the wind." One day he took a pop bottle and held it up in the wind, then quickly capped it shut. He wound up and threw the bottle (with the wind inside) as far as he could. The ceremony seemed to give him some satisfaction after he saw the bottle explode against the rocks in the canyon below.

Early in the Wandering Wheels program Davenport came to one conclusion: ride with the wind as much as possible. On their first trip down the Great River Road the summer of 1964, the riders rode most of the time against the southerly winds. Davenport soon learned that if he was to plan any more north-south trips, it would be best to start down south and ride up north.

Normally on the west-east trips, the wind is from the west —

117

to the rider's back. But that's not always the case. On their first cross-country trip from San Francisco to Rehoboth Beach, the riders had been psyched up to believe that they would have tail winds most, if not all, the way. They looked eagerly to the flatlands of Kansas, where they would not only have a tail wind, but no mountain climbing. But as it turned out, the entire trip across Kansas was spent fighting a southeast head wind.

"We've been told that the Gulf of Mexico creates a certain weather condition that makes a continual southeast wind through Kansas, Nebraska, Texas, and Oklahoma. Whatever the reason, we've found it true whenever we've crossed these states."

During one crossing, the riders had just finished drinking some lemonade a bank had served them and were ready to climb back on their bikes for the last leg of the day's trip. A sheriff came up and told Davenport that a twister had just touched down ten miles back and that the entire area was under a tornado warning.

The tornado, of course, creates a west wind, and the bike riders had been bucking that southeast wind all the way across Kansas. When the wind began blowing, Davenport couldn't hold his guys back. The wind began howling steadily in excess of thirty miles per hour, and the guys climbed back on their bikes and headed out. They put their bikes in high gear and shot for the next town, about thirty-five miles away. They rode with lightning to their backs, with thunder clapping overhead, and with the wind behind them. It was a foolhardy thing to do, but the guys looked at it as a "gift from God." They made the next town in less than an hour.

Davenport had high hopes that on their 1969 trip from Miami to Seattle the Wheels wouldn't encounter the strong Kansas headwinds. But the wind still seemed against them as they cut across the state from the southeast to the northwest. "It seems that if we decided to turn around in the middle of our trip and head back to where we started," Davenport says, "the wind would shift too, just to work against us."

Davenport has coined a phrase that he uses on the riders during an especially hard day of riding against the wind. He says, "You guys know from experience that there is a good wind and a bad wind; the difference is in the direction you're going." Of course,

Davenport is using the wind as an analogy of life, and it doesn't take long for the guys to catch on.

Another thing the Wheels soon learned early in their cycling tours was to get rid of the fenders on their bikes. Fenders are for keeping water off the rider when he's riding. But when you're riding a bike in the rain, it doesn't do much good. To get wet as one of the Wandering Wheels is to get all wet, so why carry along the extra weight of fenders?

Rain, as always, is a source of irritation. It's bad, in the first place, because it makes it more difficult for the drivers to see the riders. Normally, in a heavy rain the riders will stop. But if they are stuck out in the middle of nowhere, there is not much else they can do but ride.

Rain also makes the road slippery, making it difficult for the riders to control their bikes. More important, when the rims get wet, the clincher brakes cannot stop the bike.

The Wandering Wheels have encountered some real downpours. If they have been riding on a hot day, a rain can be fun. On one Miami to Seattle trip, after a hot morning, there was a torrential downpour and the riders welcomed the rain like a bunch of dolphins. The gutters were filled to the curbs, and at one point Davenport spotted a group who had jumped off their bikes and lain down in the gutter, the water rushing over and past them to the sewers.

Normally, however, rain is a discomfort. The Wandering Wheels have no rain gear. Everything they wear is porous, so if it rains, the riders get soaked to the skin. If they have too many rainy days in a row, they stop at a laundromat to dry out their things. "One of the most comfortable feelings is to have your old bones all wet," Davenport says, "and then to put on warm clothes just out of the dryer. It's a great sensation."

Riding through Ohio in 1969 the riders had encountered several days of rain. When they got near Wooster, they came to a bridge that had earlier been washed out. All traffic was being detoured, but the creek under the road had since dropped in level to about ankle deep.

Instead of following the detour the riders decided to wade across the gulley and continue their ride on the other side. There were little "islands" on which they could step, so it was a relatively easy venture.

On the other side, however, the riders found a fence blocking them from the road. One of the riders, Bill Howison, climbed over first. Once on the other side, he reached over the fence to have his bike handed to him and brushed up against the fence. He jumped back. "Hey! That's electric!" he said.

He thought the next guy to come over, Lee Black, had heard him, but for some reason his comment hadn't registered. When Lee lifted his bike and leaned over to pass it across the fence, he also leaned against the fence. The current surged through his body and he threw his bike into the air. "Yeow!" he screamed, and for the next few moments he was jumping around making a big fuss over the shock he had been given. Of course, he really wasn't hurt, and the other guys finally coaxed him over the fence to the other side so they could continue their trip.

"... on a hot day. ..."

Davenport has also found the rain to be a source of inspiration. Coming into Savannah, Georgia, during the 1967 tour, he ran into a bad storm. He was on his motorcycle, in front of the riders by about twenty miles, looking for a place to stay that night.

The rain was blowing horizontally to the ground. Davenport was nearly blown off his bike. He was concerned about the guys behind him, wondering if they had found some shelter.

120

Davenport took shelter under the interstate highway bridge until the rain finally diminished. After it was over, he quickly rode into town and found the Baptist church in which the riders would spend the night. He then rode back to meet the fellows. To his amazement they were dry.

"Hey, where did you guys sit out the storm?" he asked.

"What storm?" the others asked. The rain had just missed them.

While he had been waiting out the storm under the highway bridge, Davenport had been thinking of the words to a song the Wheels had been singing in their concerts. A phrase, "I'll just keep trusting the Lord as I ride along," had kept running through his mind. When he met up with the guys, he knew how much those words really meant to him and the other Wandering Wheels.

Sometimes with the rain will come hail, and according to Davenport, there is hardly anything worse. The Wheels have been hit by hail only three or four times during their first six years of touring. One night on the 1968 trip the Wheels got word that there were tornado warnings out. They pitched camp and set up their tents, mostly to keep off the mosquitoes, but also just in case it rained.

Six or seven fellows were squashed into each tent, two or three were in the truck in their sleeping bags, and five or six others were in the trailer. The remainder slept underneath the truck, and some in the men's john.

Sure enough, that night it started to rain. And then the wind began to blow. And finally, it began to hail! "We had our windows down on the tent," says Davenport. "There was some screening there, but the hail was real intense, and we tried to zip up the zipper to keep it from breaking in. As we did, the hail pounded our knuckles so hard that the next morning some of the guys' hands were bruised.

"That night, one of our real interesting characters, Val Stevens, was sleeping in the trailer. Val had a habit of nightwalking, or just bolting up in bed and yelling out some outlandish phrase. Of course he was always fun to sleep with, because you didn't know what to expect from him in the middle of the night.

"Val had taken the one place in the trailer that night that he

121

shouldn't have. He slept about eight inches from the top of the thin aluminum shell. When the hail came pounding down, he woke with a start — the hail beating just inches above him. He awoke screaming and hollering."

Val woke up the whole camp, screaming, "Help! Get me outa here! Help! Help!"

Davenport ripped the door of his tent trying to get out and to the trailer as fast as he could. Everybody in the camp was spooked with Val's screaming.

Both the cooks were in the back of the truck, and they forgot that the door had been closed. One of them, Herb Boyd, jumped out of his sleeping bag and ran right into the door.

Underneath the trailer, Gary Jones sat up with a start and bumped his head on the bottom of the trailer. The camp was in utter chaos.

"We all reached the trailer door about the same time," Davenport tells. "We flung open the door and yelled out, 'What's wrong?' Val said very quietly, 'Nothing's wrong. The hail just woke me.' "

Perhaps the most difficult weather condition the riders have to confront is the humidity. In areas close to large bodies of water, the riders sweat profusely. Particularly in Georgia, the Wandering Wheels find that they have to depend heavily on salt tablets to replenish their salt supply. In some cases, Davenport has seen the riders' red jackets turned white from the salt in the riders' perspiration.

Cold weather is never a major problem; it's always the hot weather. Originally, Davenport had the riders take along sweat clothes to protect them from the cold mornings, but he soon found that they were being used more to protect the riders from the sun.

The rider's leg action causes his thigh to be parallel to the ground most of the time and perpendicular to the sun. There is no other part of the body that receives more of the direct rays of the sun than the thigh.

"Our riders have taken a real beating in this area," Davenport says. "It will burn and blister and chap. So we designed a little patch to draw up over the thigh, to protect it. We usually use a nylon piece that isn't as heavy as normal sweat clothing. It is

122

light in weight, yet gives the rider the comfort of keeping the sun off this part of his body."

Hats or caps are also important to the Wandering Wheels rider for warding off the sun. The riders all want to wear their own particular style of hat, so rather than buying a standard hat for the Wandering Wheels, Davenport has let them choose their own.

A Wandering Wheel's hat runs from a simple golf hat with the bill, to engineer caps, to baseball caps. Hats with large bills would really do a better job, but such hats are not in vogue, and the wind tends to blow them off.

The baseball cap seems to have done the best job of keeping the sun off the nose and lips. Of course, any hat will keep the sun from baking the top of the head. Some Wandering Wheels have had to change the parts in their hair during a trip because they've been in the sun too long.

"The worst place to ride in the sun is, of course, in the desert," says the Wandering Wheels director. "And an added chore of desert riding is that the fellas have to get up earlier. We figure this is the only way to make it across the desert, though. We ride early in the day before the heat gets intense.

"We get a little added blessing getting up before the sun. The guys stumble around in the darkness, not sure why or where they are going. It's kind of romantic to sit there having our devotions as the sun is starting to come up. You wouldn't want to do it every day, but it does add an extra bit of romance to the trip."

The weather nearly sidelined the Taylor coach on one of the early Wandering Wheels trips. In 1966 the riders had spent the night in a Little League park in Hebron, Ohio. They had moved their equipment and tents down into a little gully for the night and set up camp. That night it rained, and when the troupe woke up in the morning, some of them were floating on their air mattresses.

The night before, Davenport had moved the truck down into the gully with them, so it would be close by. That morning when they tried to pull it out, it got stuck. Davenport pushed and shoved with the others, trying to free it from the mud, and in the process wrenched his back.

They finally got the truck back on the road, and the fellows put

123

Davenport on his bike and headed him in the right direction. "I rode all that day," Davenport remembers. "I would rather have died right there on the highway than to have gotten that far on the trip and not have been able to complete it."

Such are the hardships of the Wandering Wheels caused by all kinds of weather. Yet there are still more —

16

"What do Christians do for excitement?"

Hillclimbing: the hill or mountain or anything up is work for the cyclist. The Wandering Wheels haven't found it any different. "A rider will feel a 1 percent grade," says Davenport. "He'll feel the level ground. What we have learned about hillclimbing is to relax while you're going up that grade. A hill can wipe you out physically, if you're not careful."

Russ Lesser, a Wandering Wheels alumnus who first traveled with the 1966 team and again in 1970, describes climbing the Sierras on a bike this way: "The first part of your body that tires is your legs: you've been pushing with them. Then your back and shoulders begin to hurt, because you've been pumping with your whole body. You get pains in your chest and in your sides. Your breathing gets heavier, but weaker. Half-way up, your mind begins to play tricks on you. The ground looks flat, but it's still a grade. As you near the top it feels like someone has put a thousand-pound weight on your chest. You just keep going anyway, knowing that if you stop, you're finished."

Hopefully, the Wandering Wheels rider has done his homework back in Upland, Indiana, before heading for the West Coast to begin his trip. One of the primary reasons for using the ten-speed derailleur bike in the program is to allow, through various gear combinations, a steady and even pedaling pace. If the rider is not well-acquainted with his gears before the trip, he will be using much more of his own power than necessary to climb those hills.

125

"A rider will feel a 1 percent grade."

To ensure easy shifting and to avoid damaging the derailleur, the rider should be acquainted with the following pointers: first, he should shift only when the wheels and pedals are in motion; second, he should ease up on the pedals while shifting; third, he should shift only one or two steps at a time; fourth, he shouldn't shift when the bicycle is stationary or coasting; fifth, he shouldn't shift while applying heavy pressure on the pedals; sixth, he shouldn't pedal backwards while shifting; and seventh, he should never force the shifting gear.

The shift levers are located on both sides of the handlebar stem. As the rider pedals along, the lever on his right controls the rear derailleur. To shift into low gear — to climb a hill — the rider pulls the right hand lever towards the rear of the bicycle. When the chain is positioned on any particular rear sprocket, the gear can be lowered by shifting the front derailleur. Pushing the left hand lever towards the front of the bicycle will accomplish this.

To shift into high gear — for greater forward speed — the rider merely pushes the right hand lever towards the front of the bike. Pulling the left hand lever towards the rear of the bike will make the gear higher.

Remembering all these points is understandably confusing to the novice rider of a derailleur bicycle. Those Wandering Wheels who ride the shorter trips or who ride on the Miami to Seattle tours have the advantage of experience behind them before they tackle those tough mountain ranges.

Those who ride the west to east coast-to-coast trips aren't so lucky. "I think our toughest hill is the Priest grade in the mountainous area just east of San Francisco," says Davenport. "We've been told that many trucks are routed around that particular area not necessarily because of its steepness, but because of its length."

The road winds up the mountain range for about forty miles. During the 1968 Wheels trip, one of the riders was heard commenting at the end of his climb, "Man, I was afraid I was going to die!" To which another Wheel complained, "Man, I was afraid I wasn't going to die!"

Most of the riders have found that the best way to climb any hill is to gear down as low as they can and forget about going anywhere fast. They relax and take the pedaling as it comes. The riders don't see much when they are climbing a hill. They concentrate on their front wheels and the patch of pavement around it. On the steeper hills, when traffic permits, they zig-zag up the grade, cutting down the percentage. It lengthens the ride, but it eases the pedaling.

In the Wandering Wheels it's a cardinal sin to get any help from anybody. You're to do it all by yourself. If anyone is caught cheating, he is usually slapped down.

On their Miami to Seattle journey in 1969, the riders had been bucking a headwind all morning coming out of Atwood, Kansas. Davenport was on the motorcycle riding up behind the packs, trying to get ahead of them before lunch. A couple of riders flagged him down and asked, "Did you see those guys in the pick-up truck?"

"No, I didn't. Do you mean there are a couple of our guys riding in the back of a truck?"

"Yeah, they sure are, and we're really honked off about it. Here we are tearing our guts out, killing ourselves, and these guys are spoiling what we are trying to do. They're cheatin', and they're a bad example for the group!"

Davenport was hopping mad. He jumped back on his motorcycle and roared up the road in hot pursuit. When he found them, they were back on their bikes riding.

"Hey!" he shouted. "Stop!" After he pulled them over, he asked, "Did you guys hitch a ride in a truck back there?"

The two guys looked at each other. "Yeah, we did."

"Why! Don't you know what you were doing to the guys who saw you go by?"

"Well . . . the guy offered us a ride, and . . . we thought it would be sort of fun to ride past the fellas and wave, I guess . . ."

"Well, then, let me invite you to climb aboard those bikes of yours and ride those miles over again!" Davenport was still angry. "And if you two think you'd rather not do that, we'll get you a couple of plane tickets so you can go home in the morning!"

The two riders knew they had done wrong and were sorry. The Wandering Wheels truck took them back to where they had hitched the ride, and they pedaled back over the distance they had cheated on.

But even the leaders have fudged a bit when the opportunity, you might say, "rolled past." On the second Wandering Wheels trip through the North Central states, Davenport was riding with two other fellows up a West Virginia hill. It was late in the afternoon, and the day had been long.

As they slowly pedaled forward, along came a slow moving semitrailer truck, inching its way up the hill. The temptation was too great. "We just reached out and grabbed onto that truck and got pulled all the way to the top," the coach confesses. "I found myself feeling a little guilty after that — say, for about two or three minutes."

Davenport learned early in the Wandering Wheels program that it's best to stop at the top of a hill and not at the bottom. "If our break comes at the bottom of a hill, our fellas would rather ride to the top first, even if they're dog-tired. They don't want to tackle a hill first thing after a rest."

Even if someone's bike breaks down on the way up a hill, the rest of the riders keep going. It's important to keep moving and not to break stride, they have discovered. And if you're ever looking for the Wandering Wheels at a rest stop when you're in the hills, you'll usually find them at the top.

On their first cross-country trip, the Wheels hit the foothills of the Sierras in the late afternoon. They had had a late lunch that day, and being inexperienced at bicycle touring, had decided to camp at the top, not realizing that they were going to try to accomplish this feat at the worst time of day.

In addition to starting their climb in the late afternoon, the altitude would affect them.

Davenport was riding a bike in the pack, and at first they all had a lot of ecstasy — these were their first "mountains" and their first mountain climb. Before long, however, all that zeal faded. Most of the riders were finding it an impossible task. It was beginning to get dark and many of the riders were feeling desperate.

At regular intervals you could see one of the Wandering Wheels fagged out along the highway. Some were pushing their bikes. Others were sitting alongside the road.

"We learned that you don't take off in the afternoon without much of a food supply in your stomach and without really knowing how far you plan to go," says Davenport. "I vowed at the beginning of that trip that I would ride that bike across America and that I wouldn't get off and walk. But I walked about one hundred feet of that thirty-six hundred miles. I was so tired I had no trouble admitting defeat."

When Davenport reached the top, the truck had already arrived and had unloaded the sleeping bags into one large heap. He just sprawled out on top of those bags and fell into a deep sleep. "I think I just disappeared inside those bags and fell into a world you couldn't compare with any drug trip," he recalls.

One thing the Wandering Wheels don't have to worry about when hillclimbing is an accident. Davenport can't recall a single accident occurring while going up a hill. The riders are going too slowly to get into any serious trouble. It's a different story going down.

For the Wandering Wheels, the most dangerous aspect of bicycling is coasting down the mountains. "I think I shudder most about the fellas when they're coasting," says Davenport. He knows from experience that the most serious accidents have occurred on the downhill glides.

The Wandering Wheels have been clocked at speeds up to sixty-five miles per hour downhill. "We don't encourage this," says Davenport, "but now and then we allow a few of the more experienced riders to go."

Davenport spreads the riders out about a quarter of a mile apart. Then he lets the first rider head down the grade and waits until he feels he's safely ahead. "We don't want the rider behind plowing into a kid if he's had a wreck," Davenport explains. Then he says, "Okay, Jones; you're next!" and shoves off the second rider down the chute.

"It's kind of a bone-chilling experience," says Davenport, who reached an estimated fifty or sixty miles per hour during the 1966 trip. "You come in and out of the shadows as you round one corner, then another."

Unless the rider falls, he doesn't have to worry much about motor traffic behind him. Usually, the cyclists can maneuver the switchbacks much better than a driver. They do, however, have to watch for traffic ahead. Sometimes cars coming up a mountain will cut a corner, competing for the cyclist's lane. And then there was the instance when one of the cyclists overtook a Volkswagen going downhill and passed it up. "Was that driver ever shocked," says Davenport. "And we were getting better mileage."

Russ Lesser was scared, to put it bluntly, coasting down the Sierras. "I'm sure I was going top speed," he remarks. "I was afraid to use my brakes."

While pedaling up a mountain can dull a rider's spirits, coasting down the other side can zoom those spirits. To coast half the distance you've climbed is worth it, the riders say. The Wheels' longest coast has been thirty-five miles out of the Sierras into Reno, Nevada. It was so long a coast that some of the riders felt tired. Often they will coast two men abreast. "We don't mind that," Davenport says. "It's kind of fun to coast down together and talk about the things you see on the way down."

As the two coast, often one rider will pull ahead and the other

130

will drop behind to use the first man as a wind break. A little vacuum is formed behind the lead rider so that the second rider can actually increase his speed enough to pull ahead. Then the lead man drops behind and slip-streams.

When a rider is going to pass he calls out "Passing on the right!" or "Passing on the left!" When two riders are coasting together and another rider wants to pass between them, he yells, "Hey-diddle-diddle; right down the middle!"

On their 1968 tour, the Wandering Wheels were making their way into Death Valley and came into the first of two valleys. The first was called Panamint Springs. The riders coasted over several miles of barren terrain, the switchback road taking them deeper and deeper below sea level.

At the base of the valley the temperatures ranged between 115 and 120 degrees that day. It was so hot that the air-conditioned restaurant could only get its temperature down to 95 degrees, and even that felt rather refreshing, the riders said.

They got into Panamint Springs about 11:30 that morning. There was nothing there for shade but sparsely-leafed trees, and the drinking water was warm. Davenport screwed the hose onto a water pipe to hose the guys off, but there was little breeze to evaporate the moisture. The fellows tried to sleep, but they couldn't.

Davenport had decided to stay in Panamint Springs about five hours, so that they could miss riding in the extreme heat of the day. The fellows sat around reading magazines and talking to the natives.

At five o'clock that evening, after chow, the riders began to head across the valley. It was about fifteen miles to the base of the next mountain, which separated them from Death Valley. The mountain was about four thousand feet above sea level, and though Davenport hadn't known this at the time, the road is the steepest state road in the United States.

As they started out, the temperature had dropped to about 100 degrees. The riders put on their white shirts and their blinking lights so they could be seen by passing motorists, and instead of sending the equipment truck ahead, which had become the practice, the truck trailed behind, flashing its lights. One of the motorcycles led the pack; the other shepherded the group along the side.

The ride across the valley floor was comfortable. They had no trouble at all. It was an interesting ride, says Davenport, because the floor was covered with unusual growth and with rocks that moved mysteriously. Finally, they reached the base of the mountain and started climbing. But the grade was too steep and the riders had to get off their bikes and walk them.

In the mountains and the valleys the night drops quickly around you. Instead of keeping the riders spread apart, the leaders ganged them together. They moved up the grade pushing their bikes with the lights blinking to ward off any motorist who might come up from behind.

The higher they climbed that night, the cooler it turned, giving the riders the promise of something better at the top.

After six hours of work, they finally reached the summit. On the entire trip up only about ten cars had passed, many drivers no doubt wondering what a strange sight to see in the middle of the night.

"We couldn't see anything," Davenport recalls. "There were no lights. No moon or stars, either. But we knew that Death Valley lay below us."

The riders gathered in a parking lot at the summit, and a few of them scraped away a few of the rocks and lay down. Davenport and the other leaders planned their next move.

He knew there was a ranger station somewhere part way down the mountain and decided to try to find it. He knew that if he could get the riders down far enough that night, they wouldn't have so long a ride the next morning down into Death Valley. He took the Triumph and headed down the mountain.

"Riding all alone in the dark, with only the sound of your motorcycle, and only the light of a small headlamp was a unique experience," says Davenport. "I made it down to the ranger station with no trouble and arranged for a place for the fellas to sleep that night."

Davenport then rode back up the mountain to where he had left the others. What was to come about the next hour was perhaps the most harrowing experience the riders ever had. "We got together the first group and put the convertible behind them and one motorcycle in front of them. We told them that the road was about a 13 percent grade, so they should be careful not to get going too fast.

"It was still warm, and the men began coasting down toward the ranger station. As they were going down, the fellas would suddenly disappear from view of the convertible's headlights, then they'd reappear as they came out of the dip in the road. When they rounded a curve, it was the same thing: they would disappear in the darkness until the convertible could position itself again directly behind them."

The riders were traveling about thirty-five or forty miles per hour down the mountainside, with only a motorcycle with a single-beam light leading the way, and a convertible which constantly lost sight of them. There they were, in total darkness, coasting down the mountain, braking, coasting, following the motorcycle, tailed by a convertible, its lights disappearing as they dipped into a valley or screamed around a curve, straining every nerve and muscle in their bodies, trying to concentrate on the darkness before them.

Suddenly, some of the riders encountered a new problem: without being aware of it, the riders had been using their brakes more than usual. Their rims were beginning to heat up and their tires were starting to blow.

The Wandering Wheels leaders made that trip three times that night, and despite the blown tires, all the riders were brought down safely to the ranger station. Waiting for the next morning, when their speed wouldn't have been hindered by darkness, could have meant a serious accident, Davenport feels.

That evening as one of the groups was coasting down the mountain, one of the riders, Bobby Diller, was coasting down alongside the lead motorcycle. Like nearly half of all Wandering Wheels riders, Bobby had come from a conservative Christian home where Christianity had offered little excitement. Bobby, a fine athletic specimen — muscles on top of muscles — was riding down alongside Murf, enjoying every tense moment of it, not knowing when a rabbit would scoot across the road or a chuck hole would suddenly appear.

As they were sailing together and talking, Bobby turned to Murf and said, "Hey, Murf, what do Christians do for excitement, anyway!"

It was his way of saying, "Who says Christians don't have any fun?" It was a response characteristic of what Davenport hoped the Wandering Wheels program was trying to show.

17

"When I consider Thy heavens...."

Davenport is convinced of the desirability of linking spiritual meditation and practice with physical activity in a relaxed or unstructured situation. On the 1965 trip through the North Central states the group was getting ready to eat lunch one day, and Davenport called the riders together under a large tree beside the road and asked who'd like to pray. The fellows all kept their heads down and didn't move, fearful that any movement or eye contact might indicate that they were volunteering. Finally, the leader called on one of them.

The fellow started praying as many teen-agers would — awkwardly and meaninglessly — and rambled on with the usual stock phrases you might associate with prayer before meals.

Davenport, meantime, was getting restless. And when the fellow prayed, "and bless the hands that have prepared this food," Davenport barked, "Stop that prayer!"

Immediately, everyone looked up with shock on their faces.

"Do you know what you just said?" Davenport said to the young man who was praying.

"What?"

"You asked God to bless Bob's hands." Davenport called to Bob Uhrich, their cook, and asked him to come over to where they were standing. "Bob," he said to the cook. "Hold out your hands!" Uhrich held out his grubby hands. "Look at those hands," Davenport said to the riders. "Why, they don't even look clean.

But he's got strong hands. He can wield a knife as well as anybody. You've seen him whittling or sticking a blade in a tree at five paces. But when you asked God to bless his hands . . . it sounded like you were thinking of some woman's hands. Is that what you meant?"

The kid who had been praying squirmed. "No, . . . not exactly, I guess. But that's just what I heard at home . . . you know. . . ."

"Sure," said Davenport, "that's just the point. You're not home now, and your mom isn't fixing the food. Bob Uhrich, our big,

"And since we're men . . . let's start talking to God like men. . . ."

burly cook is fixing the food. Don't make him sound like a sissy. We've got to start thinking about what we are praying about. God is interested in us. He wants to hear what we want to say. And since we're men, from now on let's start talking to God like men — like we'd talk to each other."

From then on, prayer on that trip took on a new purpose and freshness — guys talking to God as they would to each other. The incident has been repeated from time to time as Davenport takes on a new crew of riders. It doesn't take more than a few lunches and a few prayers to bring out this phrase — and Davenport is always ready to expose it.

Davenport and the Wandering Wheels riders talk a great deal about the spiritual benefits of a Wandering Wheels tour. Much of what they experience spiritually, as mentioned previously, is based on their viewpoint of life and its meaning. For someone not oriented this way, many of the "blessings" the Wandering Wheels speak about would go unnoticed. If noticed, they would be regarded from a different viewpoint.

For instance, every problem Davenport and the riders confront gives a rationale for telling God about it and asking His guidance. Every good thing that happens to them is accepted as a "gift from God," and gives an opportunity to thank and give praise for it.

This attitude need not indicate any sign of weakness on the part of the Wandering Wheels or others who may believe this way. For Davenport, to go to God with a problem is to merely acknowledge his personal understanding that God controls the situation and that he (Davenport) is trusting Him (God) to work it out for the best. To thank and praise God for a particular gift, again, is merely an acknowledgment that all good things proceed from God.

People without such a view are not excluded from the same gifts. Neither are they kept from the same problems. The beauty of nature, for example, is for all people to enjoy whether they praise God for it or not — or whether they even believe there is a God. The ugliness of sin or the results of sin (such as war, for an example) is equally shared by all people — even with those who are devout.

Davenport's view of life and its ultimate purpose is a Biblical view. That's why he and his riders spend time each day reading and discussing the Bible; they are learning and applying this view to everyday situations. Those who accept a more worldly view regard life as a series of "happenings" by chance and see little purpose in living other than the immediate.

Whichever view is practiced, it is important to acknowledge the existence of the other. It is equally important to realize that it is impossible to develop a style of life that practices both views simultaneously. As Jesus once said, "No man can serve two masters: for either he will hate the one, and love the other; or else he will hold to the one, and despise the other. . . ."

Those who think or believe or act as does Davenport are mastered by their viewpoints; yet they serve that viewpoint willingly.

This is why Davenport can say, truthfully, that he is "always impressed with the wind. It can be so beautiful and, then again, so discouraging. Like the wind, is the cloud. If the kids wake up in the morning and see a cloud, they'll know that God has provided a little protection from the sun that day."

God's wonders in nature also appeal to the senses. Not that the non-Christian or the atheist is robbed of these senses, but that man with a Christian view enjoys a more personal response with his mind. "Late in the afternoon when you're riding up one knoll and down the other you can feel the change in temperature," says Davenport. "It's cooler in the valleys. You can only experience this sensation on a bicycle. Only as a Christian can you appreciate it as a gift — as a child would appreciate a surprise gift from his father. The aroma of flowers or evergreens. Even the ugly smell of a dead animal can be appreciated as a way the Creator warns his other creatures of danger.

"You become sort of a barometer, sensing the moisture and changes in weather with your skin. Coming into Yosemite in 1968 was beautiful. The fellas were coasting down the valley, rolling around one corner, then another, being introduced at each turn to more beauty. One of the riders stopped on his way down and said to me, 'You know, I really don't know if I want to go further right now; I've stored up more in my mind than I can handle; I'm afraid the rest will just run over and be wasted.' "

My cup runneth over. . . .

What that rider expressed to Davenport speaks highly of the

experience a young person can have from just riding a bicycle in the outdoors. In the desert the Wandering Wheels have found tiny flowers growing in the barren ground along the roadside — tiny flowers about one-fourth the size of a penny — a single flower or a clump of them. Everything in miniature, yet the rider is able to appreciate even more the beauty of the desert.

Speaking of Monument Valley, Arizona, Davenport says, "Man has not as yet matched the beauty of the rock formations in that place: monuments built of sandstone and storm."

At the Grand Canyon the riders were able to appreciate the years of carving done by the Colorado River, each strata of rock which the Creator had laid there in time being exposed.

In Kansas in 1966 the Wheels crossed the wheat fields just near harvest time. At one place the wind was blowing across the golden heads of grain, rippling the field like a stormy sea. "The beauty of it actually inspired us as we fought to ride against that wind," recalls Davenport.

All bodies of water — rivers, lakes, streams, the oceans — all are strangely romantic when seen from a bicycle. Each offers a spiritual dimension as well as an aesthetic appreciation, the Wandering Wheels leader says. "It's wonderful to ride along a river and watch its liveliness. It seems to be symbolic of life itself. In the more barren parts of America, you spot a row of green trees, and you know there is a river over there."

"[The godly] shall be like a tree planted by the rivers of water, that bringeth forth his fruit in his season; his leaf also shall not wither; and whatsoever he doeth shall prosper. The ungodly are not so: but are like the chaff which the wind driveth away."

"Sleeping underneath the great pines in California gives you a brand new dimension of a tree," says Davenport. "Lying back, looking up at the stars in a smog-free sky through the branches of a pine hundreds of years old is almost psychedelic!"

Rocks also impressed the riders. When the Wheels were using their original trailer, they noticed that near the end of their trip they were having a number of flat tires. The riders had been collecting rocks during the entire route and had been storing them in their lockers, causing an overload.

They were also impressed with the wild life. They found they could sneak up on a deer without much trouble when the wind was blowing against them. The bike made little noise.

Coming into Flagstaff, Arizona, on one trip, Davenport was riding the motorcycle and spotted a bobcat that had been freshly killed by a truck. Out in front of the cat was a large rat-like animal. Davenport could just imagine how the cat had been chasing the rodent across the highway just as a big truck rumbled by and struck them both.

Davenport picked up the bobcat and draping it on his motorcycle rack carried it into town to show the other riders: "It was a beautiful specimen," he explains simply.

On the second trip across the U.S. in 1967 the Wheels pulled into a small town called Twenty-nine Palms. They arrived about ten o'clock that morning, and the people in the town wouldn't let the riders continue across the valley until the angle of the sun had diminished; it was blistering hot. About noon it had rained hard in the mountains, so later in the afternoon Murf took some of the riders down to a creek bed to watch for a flash flood.

When they arrived, only a trickle of water wound down the middle of the bed, but in about ten minutes the trickle had turned into a ribbon of about four inches. In the next five minutes the river was a band three feet wide and then, suddenly, a roaring torrent twenty yards wide!

Real drama! Several of the fellows decided to go swimming. They had fun frolicking around and being carried down the river bed, though when they climbed out they were miserably dirty and full of sand.

In Salt Lake City, Utah, the riders recalled stories from their history books about the American pioneers seeing water off in the distance only to discover when they reached it that it was brackish. They could empathize with the pioneers, for they saw the same waters on the salt flats and knew they couldn't drink it.

> I will pour water upon him that is thirsty, and floods upon
> the dry ground: I will pour my spirit . . . .

At the close of the 1968 trip, the Wandering Wheels had just come over the Washington Bridge in New York City onto Manhattan Island. Davenport was riding the lead motorcycle, ahead of the group, which was the normal custom, looking for 53rd St. He had figured to find the church in which they were to stay, then circle back and rendezvous with the group.

But he hadn't realized how big New York City is, and before he knew it, he was lost.

It was about 7:30; still light; and Davenport wasn't too desperate at first, figuring that he'd just ride around until he found them. It wasn't exactly that he was lost or that they were lost; it was that they were separated from each other, and neither knew where the other was.

"I just couldn't figure how I could lose that number of bike riders wearing bright orange shirts, with orange flags on their bikes, all alike, all on one island," he remembers. "I rode around for about an hour, up one street, down the other, seeking the fellas. I finally found myself asking people if they had seen the group. Most of them responded with a look that made me feel like some kook: 'Sure, bike riders all the way from San Francisco?' I finally stopped asking.

"After an hour and a half went by, I was really desperate. I stopped at a street corner, where there was a cop, and told him my problem. 'I know this may sound funny,' I said, 'but I've got these forty kids I've led on bicycles all the way from San Francisco, and I lost them. I know you probably don't believe me, but if you happen to see them, will you tell them that they're looking for the Lexington Methodist Church on 53rd St.?' He said he would.

"He seemed to accept my story with a ho-hum attitude, and I had no confidence that he'd see these kids while standing on this one corner in the whole of New York City. But I sort of unburdened myself on him and felt that I had, at least, done all I could do to find them."

At the same time Dale Murphy was leading the riders through the city, knowing that they had been separated from Davenport and wondering what to do next. He couldn't find Davenport or the church and had come to the same conclusion — that they were lost.

About four hours later, at 11:30, he wheeled past this same corner. Later, he explained what happened: "I had come to the point that I was completely insufficient to solve the problem," he told Davenport. "I decided to admit to God that I didn't know where

142

you or the church were, and to tell Him that I was completely dependent on Him to get us back together.

"It wasn't a prayer — the kind where I got off my bike and down on my knees, or stood inside a church; it wasn't even a request that we get back together; it was just a recognition that we were completely dependent upon Him. Sort of, 'What's Your solution, God?'

"I stopped my motorcycle at this corner and was sitting there thinking about these things, pausing to say this little prayer, when suddenly I heard this voice: 'Hey! Are you looking for the church?'

"At first, I didn't think I was hearing things right, that this was all my imagination. I was actually afraid to look over in the direction of the voice for fear that it was my imagination or that there was some kind of angel standing there. I never would have been able to explain *that!*

"But when I finally looked up, there was this policeman. I got off my motorcycle and ran across the street and shook his hand like he was an angel, and he told us how to get to the church."

Murphy and Davenport and the other Wandering Wheels who experienced that situation understand there are those who would prefer to reduce the significance of the event. They don't overlook all the pieces that went into forming the whole. They don't even call it a "miracle"; a miracle cannot be explained. But they do appreciate the beauty of the Force which met their particular need.

> When I consider thy heavens, the work of thy fingers, the moon and the stars, which thou hast ordained; what is man, that thou art mindful of him, and the son of man, that thou visitest him? For thou hast made him a little lower than the angels, and hast crowned him with glory and honor.

This is how the Wandering Wheels relate the Bible to their everyday experiences.

18

"Dear Mr. Davenport. . . ."

"Dear Mr. Davenport,

"Our thanks for what you have done for our son can never truly be expressed.

"Last winter was probably one of the worst we have ever experienced as parents. He was rebellious, headstrong, undisciplined, and very mixed up emotionally. We knew he was searching [for something], but we didn't know how to help. It's a very lost feeling, when you can't help one you love so much.

"Our prayers were answered with this [Wandering Wheels] trip this summer. He is such a different person today; it's almost a miracle! . . . We are very proud of him and forever in your debt.

"He is looking forward to the trip this summer, and we will do everything possible to see that he goes. . . .

"Sincerely,"

The home office of the Wandering Wheels has received numerous such letters from parents who say that they sent a boy to them and received back a man. "The mere fact that a kid is away from his home for five weeks is some kind of a help in producing a change," Davenport suggests.

On the trips the riders see how difficult it is to work around the house. They learn to appreciate the fact that there is a lot of work around the kitchen, and when they get home, they begin to chip in, knowing how hard it can be. Several of the moms have written Davenport to thank him for teaching their sons not to make such a mess around the house. Others write about the new appreciation they receive from their sons.

Five weeks on the road, experiencing for the first time the rigors of washing his own clothes, does tend to instill a different attitude toward mom. Several fellows had never experienced washing clothes in a laundromat. A few failed to read the instructions and proceeded to dump in as much as a half a box of soap sometimes, convinced that their clothes were that dirty. And when the suds began bubbling over the top of the machine, they couldn't understand why the attendant got upset.

Separating white items from colored items was unheard of. So, the bright red jackets tinted everything else a pretty pink, leaving several embarrassed young men riding in pink shorts.

The riders also learn the value of money. "They could easily spend twenty dollars at Dairy Queens or on hamburgers," Davenport says. Some riders ran out of spending money and had to write home for more — quite embarrassed to admit that they had mismanaged what they had taken.

Food and water are other items they learn to appreciate. When they were tired and hungry they ate carrots, peas, beans, anything without complaint. Even certain foods from various sections of the country were enjoyed, although raw oysters were hard to handle.

The riders made up a joke about avocados:

"What does an avocado taste like?"

"I don't know."

"You're right!"

One young man from an upper class family, who always had had what he wanted, found himself rationing water on the desert. "If there's anything in the American tradition that you've got plenty of, it's water," says Davenport. "It's always there at the twist of a faucet. We had been riding across the desert one day and pretty nearly came to running out of water. The next day we came into an abundance of water, and the guys were just getting their fill.

"I was standing in line, waiting my turn at the pump, and this guy was standing there washing himself and messing around for the longest time. Finally, I said, 'Hey, let's go. I want some of that stuff too.' He looked up at me and said, 'Coach, I want you to

146

know that I've never appreciated water before. I just wanted to take full advantage of it.'

"That sounded like poetry to me," says Davenport. "Here was a twenty-year-old guy, letting the water run through his interlaced hands, getting an experience from water that few other people have ever had. Just plain old water was speaking to him."

Russ Lesser traveled with the Wandering Wheels in 1966 and again in 1970. In high school Russ got hurt in football, so when he went to Taylor he couldn't play. The Wandering Wheels trip appealed to him, therefore, because he was looking for another athletic avenue.

"I was also looking for a deeper spiritual commitment," he confesses. "I had had a lot of hang-ups about the church and the Christian life. I thought the trip might do me some good."

Russ learned quickly that the demands of cycling across the country would meet his athletic need: "After pedaling up the Sierras, I felt I could conquer anything." And as far as the trip's spiritual benefits: "I got a deeper appreciation of Christ — Who He is and how He relates to my daily life."

Like other Wandering Wheels riders, Russ found that he had to go beyond himself physically and spiritually to work as part of a group. On the 1966 trip, Russ was riding behind a high schooler who began fooling around on his bike on a dangerous stretch of highway. It had been hot that day, and a difficult ride, and this kind of irresponsibility aggravated him.

"He wasn't even wearing his tail patch," Russ recalls. "It was dangerous going around the blind curves, and I decided I was going to put a stop to his antics before somebody got hurt."

Russ ran the rider off the road and told him to shape up. The kid started to cry. Later, Russ met up with Davenport and told him what had happened and asked what he should do about it. Davenport told him to "just love him."

"I had been concerned about the kid," Russ admits, "but I wasn't showing it in the right way. I learned what it means to love the way Christ loved. My basic philosophy now is to love the kids I work with." On the 1970 summer trip Russ went along as one of the trip's four leaders.

Perhaps what impresses the young people the most, and what ultimately helps them to grow into adults, is the response of the

147

adult community. They have found that by participating in a difficult and challenging effort, they have gained a positive response from the adult world. As one of the Wheels puts it, "They aren't against us after all!"

"True," says Davenport, "the adult world is disappointed in some of the avenues on which today's young people travel, but our kids just seem to turn the adults on — and it impresses our kids to find adults excited to know what they are doing."

19

"Don't stop at Fernley!"

In July of 1969, the same night that Neil Armstrong was to be the first human being to step on the surface of the moon, several of the riders wanted to view the event on television. They were in a little mountain town in Idaho that evening, and so instead of continuing on to the mountain pass, they decided to wait out the moon walk in a local bar.

The moon walk, of course, experienced one delay after another, but the riders seemed to enjoy themselves sitting in the bar drinking pop and talking with the people.

Among those at the bar was a man who had long been stewed to the gills and who had spent most of the evening sleeping. But as everyone waited for that "one small step for man; one giant leap for mankind," this drunk woke up and noticed the group of riders sitting at the bar. He screwed his eyeballs together just long enough to read the inscription on one of the fellow's shirts, and exclaimed, "Well what do ya know; the Wandering Waffles!"

Hopefully, others who have met the Wandering Wheels have had a less distorted view of who they are. According to Davenport, the number of people who have gone out of their way to praise the riders has been "overwhelming" — from little store owners to people living in the back woods of America to Presidents of the United States. "Chairmen of chambers of commerce, bankers, educators, policemen, you name it," says Davenport, "these kids have given them a new hope for the future of America."

That is not to say that the Wheels have always been received with open arms. The first person Davenport can recall having responded negatively to the riders was a woman during the 1965 trip. "Obviously she was upset about something other than just the riders," he says. "We were riding up an incline on the road and she got behind us and couldn't pass. Finally, I stopped the bikes so she could pull around us; did she ever chew us out! Man, she chewed us up one side and down the other!

"Bobby Canida, one of our riders, was standing near the car, and he looked a bit shocked at the way she was talking to us. We heard her out, though. I wanted to snap right back at her, but I wouldn't have wanted to say what I was thinking; so I just swallowed my pride and leaned down and looked into the car window and said, 'Well, God bless ya, gal. Sure's been a good day. Hope everything works out for you the rest of the day.'

"Bobby commented as she drove away, 'That's an interesting way to talk back.' "

Another time, during one of the 1967 trips, the riders came into one of the typical tourist traps along the highway. They arrived just after having spent most of their daily budget on candy and malts in a town fifteen miles back. So all they were really interested is doing was getting water for their water bottles.

After the first few came in and the owner realized that they weren't going to buy anything, he told them to get out. He didn't want them in his place if they weren't going to spend their money. This bothered Davenport and the riders. As he puts it: "One bad egg like this can dampen a full day of good experiences."

Three riders on the 1969 Miami to Seattle trip received a more violent reaction to their needs. They were riding outside Toledo, Mississippi, and came upon a country store and asked the gentleman if they could use his washroom. The man said they had no running water there, so the trio bought some pop and ice cream and candy bars and went outside again.

Before getting back on their bikes, however, they looked around for a place to respond to nature and finally noticed a ditch along the road that they could step down into with a sufficient amount of privacy. But as they were in the process of relieving themselves, out came this man with a shotgun. *Bam!*

"To say the least, we were startled," says one of the three. "I had a lot of trouble getting my pants back up before he could take another shot."

When they got back to their bikes, the man gave them a lecture about morals and the kind of family heritage they had come from, while continuing to point the loaded gun.

"You have no right to chase us off public land," one of the other riders said.

"If you kids don't get out of here," the man threatened. "I'll call the cops!"

"If you call the cops, they'll take you away," another argued.

"I don't care. I've got plenty of ammunition to hold them off!"

With that remark, the guys felt they had better get out as the man advised. They hopped on their bikes and rode off in tenth gear.

One more story nearly exhausts the bad responses of people who have encountered the Wheels, says Davenport, although incidents similar to the following have happened elsewhere from time to time. "We pulled into a town and had camped out in the park that night — in Shreveport, Louisiana — and some of the local kids, who really aren't bad, but just needed someone to slap them on the bottom once in a while to show them who's boss or to teach them what is and what isn't funny, came past our camp about three in the morning hollering and screaming.

"I always told the fellas not to sweat it; and not to encourage it by reacting. 'If you show a lack of interest,' I said, 'you'll put them down anyway.'

"This time, however, they came back for a second try. And this time they threw bottles at us. The bottles broke, spewing glass on our sleeping bags and on us.

"My first reaction was to barricade the street and the next time they came by, to catch them and beat the tar out of them. Of course, I didn't think this would be consistent with the teachings of Christ. So we let them alone.

"Other ways of getting back at them passed through my mind before the night was over," admits the Wandering Wheels leader. "I thought we could get some paint and when the guys drove past again, heave a balloon full of paint at their fancy cars. But then again I had to admit that revenge is not the Christian way. In that particular situation, where we had the choice of taking it on the chin, we finally decided to turn the other cheek."

Davenport recalls being warned along the way on one of his cross-country tours not to stop in a town by the name of Fernley, Nevada. As they neared the town he told the truck driver to drive on through the town and set up camp on the other side, in that way avoiding any problems with the townspeople.

But as he was rolling through Fernley, Davenport was stopped by some of his riders who said there was a man who wanted to meet Davenport. It turned out the man was a Methodist preacher, and he invited the Wandering Wheels to spend the night in his church.

"He had been a contractor in Michigan," Davenport explains. "Somehow he felt called as a preacher to this little town. He was building his own little church building. So we decided to stay and sent someone for the truck and trailer."

That night the Wheels put on a concert to about twenty-five people. The riders stood where the choir would stand in the plain plywood church building and sang, and talked about what they were trying to accomplish by riding across the United States. But the highlight of the entire experience for the riders was when the pastor told them that just a few weeks before he had called together the men of the church to pray about a particular problem. The town had a Little League that always held its games on Sunday mornings. The pastor was trying to get a Sunday School started at that same time and found the competition too great.

In discussing the problem, the men of that little church came to the conclusion that what they really needed was to have some way to tell the people of the town that athletics was good, but that they needed to have some time for worshiping God in church. They prayed specifically that God would send them a name athlete with whom the town could identify. A few days later, up shows Davenport, two-time All-American fullback, college football coach, with forty of the most athletic guys they'd ever hope to meet, riding bikes across America. "It really impressed the guys to realize that they were genuine answers to prayer," says Davenport.

The Wheels have also sung before two former Presidents. On their 1966 tour, Davenport had hoped that perhaps his riders could meet and sing before former President Truman in Independence, Missouri. When they arrived, he discovered that it would be quite impossible to do that. However, that morning at the Truman Library, Davenport met a secret service man assigned to guard the former executive, and the man had been so impressed with the group that he arranged for the Wheels to sing for President Truman.

The next day Davenport was introduced to the former President, and then the young men sang. Truman appeared to enjoy the brief "concert," says Davenport, and when it was over commented, "Well, that's a sure way to keep kids out of trouble."

All during the 1967 trip Davenport kept saying along the way that he hoped that his riders could sing for President Johnson at the White House. Like the year before, he had made no prior arrangements. He encouraged people they met to write their congressmen about the Wandering Wheels and continually remarked to newspaper reporters that he was hoping to get in to see the President. Some people encouraged the riders; others discouraged them about the chances to see him. When still others asked Davenport if he knew if the President would be in when they arrived in Washington, Davenport had to admit that he really didn't know.

But when they arrived in the nation's capital, the President was in. In Washington the Wheels met several people who indicated that it would nearly take an act of Congress to see the President. "Out West it seemed that we were a very important group of guys," says Davenport. "But when we arrived in Washington, we learned that there were more men in Congress than the President could see in a single year if he were to see only one a day. We began to appreciate how busy he really was."

The Wheels went on to Rehoboth Beach, Delaware, without an audience. But after they arrived, Davenport received a phone call informing him that arrangements had been made for a ten-minute session with the President on the White House lawn that Friday at noon. Needless to say Davenport and his Wandering Wheels were there at the appointed time. And so was President Johnson. The young men sang for him their "Wandering Wheels Song" to the tune of "Tumblin' Tumbleweed," and the President went around and shook each man's hand.

Davenport hopes the riders will be able to sing for other Presidents in the future.

A group of roaming youths coming into any town tends to send chills up and down the spines of much of America's adult citizenry. The contrast between the Wandering Wheels and other groups of

153

youths is referred to in nearly every newspaper account about the group. A reporter with the *Tampa Tribune* began his story this way:

> Thirty-five kids from Taylor University in Upland, Indiana, brought their demonstration to Tampa Saturday, but Police Chief J. G. Littleton didn't have to double his force, the National Guard wasn't called out, there were no big, black headlines or ugly pictures, and the town wasn't relieved when they left.
>
> They weren't dressed oddly. Instead, they were clean-cut American kids. . . .

It should be noted that these young people don't go out of their way to appear "clean-cut" or to be the adult generation's ideal of American youth. Neither do they try to capitalize on their appearance. They are still young enough and close enough to their peers to realize that outward appearances don't mean much in the nitty-gritty of life. If they appear like the more conservative element of American society, that's because they prefer to look that way — not because they are instructed to look that way in order to win a popularity contest with the people they meet. They hold to a Biblical principle that man may look on the outward appearance, but God looks on the heart. If there are any points to be earned, that's where they really count, according to the Wandering Wheels.

Winning "points" for what they are rather than for what they may look like at a given time was vividly portrayed during the Miami to Seattle trip in 1969. The Wheels were headed up into the Cascades toward a little town known as Cashmere, Washington.

For the last three hundred miles they had been seeing signs advertising a roadside stand called Tiny's. "I found myself being psyched up for the place," says Davenport. " 'Tiny's has fruit.' 'Tiny's has chicken.' 'Visit Tiny's Place.' All these signs seemed to indicate that we hadn't lived unless we'd been to Tiny's."

Davenport was the first to pull into the place, since he was leading the pack on the scout motorcycle. It had been a good day, and he was feeling a bit cocky as he rolled into a parking space out front. He was decked out in his $35 motorcycle riding jacket, wearing his blue, speckled riding helmet, dressed in his powder-blue levi pants, and wearing riding boots.

He was riding a Harley XLH motorcycle, which had saddle bags

155

on either side. He really looked the part of a cyclist. The stand was about a block long; one of the most attractive roadside stands that he had ever seen. The place was kept clean and well-manicured.

"Tiny's business thrived on car traffic, and he tried to keep the place, particularly the parking lot, receptive. He had a lot for trailers in the back, so they wouldn't take up room at the entrance. I pulled my motorcycle in where the cars were to pull in, and parked it. As I was getting off, a boy ran out of the store and said, 'Hey, Mister. Move your motorcycle; it's taking up three car places.'

"I was smart enough to know that no motorcycle could take up that much room, even if you took it all apart and scattered the parts around.

"I was feeling kind of frisky, so I gave it no thought. I jumped back on my motorcycle and moved it out to the other end of the lot."

Davenport continued to be impressed with the place as he made his way across the lot and finally into the store. As he stepped inside he suddenly wondered whose idea it was that his motorcycle was taking up three places, so he decided to ask. "Hey," he asked. "Just whose estimate was it that my motorcycle was taking up three spaces?"

Remember, even though Davenport was in a good mood and he half-jokingly asked the question, not really wanting to put anyone down, he did give the appearance of some kind of an ornery guy at first, particularly being dressed for riding a motorcycle. His appearance, therefore, was working somewhat against him.

Before he finished speaking his question, a "wall of humanity" — as he calls it — responded to his question. "Tiny had had a bad day," Davenport explains. "I obviously hit him smack dab at the wrong time. I don't know who had gotten to him earlier, but when I asked my question, he let out with a barrage of cuss words that just didn't stop. It must have gone on for forty-five seconds to a minute.

"He used cuss words upside down and backwards and end to end. My ears were just burning. I'd never been cussed out like that before. He called me all sorts of names, and of course, my chivalrous attitude and puritan life style recoiled 100 percent. I

156

found myself feeling completely justified for wanting to haul off and pound this guy in the mouth. It just burned inside me.

"After a time Tiny stopped — to get a breath, I guess — and I was flustered enough that I wasn't the coolest character in town. When he paused, I came back at him with something like, 'Mister, that's not a very nice way to talk!' Not very original, but I put all the sneer I could into it.

"That really impressed him. He just turned around and began using the same cuss words all over again."

Davenport says he knows Tiny used the same words because he had used all the world's cuss words in his first harangue. Davenport got hotter and hotter and madder and madder and began to look around for something with which to hit the man. "I wanted to explode," says Davenport, "I know that if I hadn't been a man who had embraced the Christian faith, I would have done something very foolish.

"Instead, God comforted my spirit, and as a result of my own understanding of Christ's teachings, I cooled off enough to see that I needed to swallow my pride and walk out of that store."

Davenport went back to his motorcycle and sat down. He didn't want to appear weak, yet on the other hand, he didn't want to deny by his reaction all he was trying to teach on the trip. He wanted to impress this big hunk of a man who was obviously misnamed — Tiny — with the spirit of Christ.

Five minutes later as he was still waiting for the riders to wheel into the parking lot and half-waiting for some solution to the confrontation he had had with Tiny, Davenport spotted the man coming toward him. Davenport felt for sure the man was going to tell him to get off his property. Then what would he do? The riders had been anticipating this place for the last three hundred miles.

Tiny walked up to Davenport and said, "I'm sorry." Davenport felt like crawling. "I don't know what got into me," Tiny continued, "Will you forgive me?"

Davenport says, "I was so thankful that God had given me a solution to this situation. If I had hit him, I would have been sorry to this day."

In the next few minutes Davenport explained who he was and what he was doing. "Tiny," he said, "I've got forty men who have pedaled from Miami — on the road the past four and a half weeks.

They're the finest men you'll ever see. A real compliment to America."

Tiny said he was glad to hear that. He was fed up with the hippie element in America. (Davenport later learned that the day before he had ripped a door off a hippie's car and tossed it up on the hood, and scared the youth off his property.)

Tiny called out one of his helpers and told him to break out seventeen gallons of the best juices they had. Then he asked Davenport what they had planned for dinner. Davenport said they thought they'd camp down the road.

"Would you mind if I fed you?" Tiny asked the Wandering Wheels leader. "In forty-five minutes, I'll give you all the chicken you can eat." Davenport said okay.

"When the men showed up, they couldn't believe it," he says. "They drank apple cider, cherry juice, orange juice until they were nearly sick. They downed all seventeen gallons in fifteen-ounce glasses with little chips of ice. You'd have to go a long way to equal that! The chicken was the finest chicken in the world — all respects to Colonel Sanders."

Tiny has become one of Davenport's (and the Wandering Wheels') best friends. A week later when Davenport was leading a second group of riders from Seattle to Washington, D.C., Tiny came out on the road to meet them and to invite them for dinner.

20

"Girls can't do that!"

As Davenport continued to promote his Wandering Wheels program, he began to find himself surrounded by wide-eyed teen-age girls asking when they could go along on such a tour. He joked with them: "Girls can't do that," he'd say, "That wouldn't be very feminine." But as the girls kept prodding him after film presentations about the program, he got to believing that they really would like to go and would like to sweat, and sleep on the ground. And when it came right down to thinking about a girls' tour, Davenport had to admit that they were just as capable of proving a point as were the fellows.

"I put the idea in the back of my head and slept on it," Davenport tells. "I also began to think about how often the church and other social agencies arrange programs and activities for the guys — thinking that the moms will take care of the girls, thinking that the girls don't need the attention or the adventure."

Davenport had bought a bike for his wife Barbara in 1968 and she had grown to love to ride. And as his own daughters began to grow up, Davenport came to accept the fact that the girls could do it.

At Taylor University students have what is called "Inter-term" during the month of January. The time is spent for special classes for underclassmen, but upperclassmen are free to study or work — or travel. Davenport decided he would give a girls' bike tour a trial

". . . strictly a girls' tour."

run, so in January of 1969 he led a group of twenty girls and fifteen guys on the Wandering Wheels' first coed trip.

Of course there is no better place to ride bikes in the middle of winter than Florida. Davenport found sufficient interest among the women students at Taylor to merit the trial trip. He lined up special clothing for the girls, gave them all the necessary preliminary instructions, and hauled them down to Savannah, Georgia, in a bus to begin the trip from a Baptist church pastored by Forrest Lanier, a minister the Wheels had met during the 1967 U.S. crossing.

This was strictly a girls' tour. The guys just went along to coach and to protect the girls along the way. The plan was to ride from Savannah to Jacksonville, to Miami, to Tallahassee, to Tampa. About nine hundred miles in eighteen days at approximately fifty miles a day.

"I had a good feeling about the trip," Davenport recalls. "I really felt they could make it. But when I saw them piling into the bus, I had my first misgivings. They brought hairdryers, wigs, clothes on hangers, special shoes, cosmetics. How were they going to fit all that into their little lockers? Some of them weighed less than a hundred pounds. I had been concerned enough about putting hefty guys on the highway to fight with semis. Now I was much more concerned about these frail fillies."

Davenport was so shook up about it, that when they arrived in Savannah, he took the girls to a parking lot so they could practice riding the bikes a full day before they got on the road. "My fears were confirmed," he said. "Some of them didn't even know where the brakes were. I just had to say in earnest, 'God, this is Your trip from here on out.'" The next morning the girls were off on Highway 17 to a shaky start.

"The gals had guts," says Davenport. "The trip convinced me that girls are, pound for pound, as tough as guys."

Davenport quickly learned that when you put a girl on a bike and have her pedaling along the highway, she'll sweat just like a guy. Once he remarked that the girls were sweating, and he was promptly corrected, "We don't call it sweating, Coach; we call it glowing."

"Whatever you may call it," says Davenport, "when a girl sweats or glows, she stinks just like a guy."

Davenport also learned that the guys and gals had no trouble living closely together on the trip. Before the girls went on the trip, Davenport told them to be sure to bring night clothes in which they could parade in front of the fellows without feeling embarrassed. "These kids were a real treat to work with," says Davenport. "None of them were suggestive in dress or manner. Both the guys and the gals acted honorably toward each other."

The girls and the fellows usually slept on the same floor each night, but the girls would sleep on one side of the room and the fellows on the other. In a gymnasium Davenport made half-court the dividing line. "We had some engaged couples who wanted to sleep next to each other, but my wife and I didn't think that was a good idea. The kids would connive so that the guy would sleep on one side of the half-court line and the gal on the other side. But we made a rule that they had to sleep head to head."

The Wandering Wheels leaders never wanted to break the spirit of the young people in the matter of legitimate relationships of the sexes. Sex was elevated to its proper place for both the girls and the fellows. Each seemed to have an understanding of the basic differences and limitations of the other, Davenport says. "We found this close relationship an intelligent way to teach sex, without going out of our way to get caught up in some of the hang-ups some people have about sex."

Two coeds from Taylor — Marilyn Hay, a junior, and Diane Lundquist, a senior — went along on that first Wandering Wheels coed tour. Marilyn had been Taylor Homecoming Queen — "all personality, eyes sparkly, always a smile on her face," says Davenport. She tells her own story:

"The whole purpose of the girls' trip was different from that of the guys'. It was more recreational and social than athletic, I guess you'd say. I suppose the guys thought we had it soft, but I'd never been so tired physically before.

"Yet, God got me through the trip by giving me more determination. I found I had more strength in me than I had thought. I found the trip exhilarating!

"The trip made me feel a sense of accomplishment, and it gave me the prestige I wanted as a Wandering Wheel.

"We had a destination each day, and we always stayed inside at night — usually in gyms and churches. If it was a gym, we'd make a mad scramble for the wrestling mats. The first there got to sleep on them that night. And when we were to sleep in a church the guys would race the gals for the upstairs, where there usually was carpeting.

"I guess what climaxed the trip for me was my accident. We had just left Clearwater, Florida, and had the choice of riding this final leg of the trip on a bus — it was raining — or on our bikes. Some of the guys wanted to take the bus the last twenty-five miles, but the girls were unanimous — we wanted to ride our bikes. So we all rode.

"Coach warned us about the dangers of the last day. He reviewed the safety rules with us and told us to ride carefully. We took off in packs of six or seven with a couple of city blocks between packs.

"I was in the second group. The first group came upon this bridge and safely pedaled across, and then our group started to

162

head across it. A boy was leading our group to break the wind, and suddenly his tire skidded on the iron grating and he went down.

"He was only a few inches in front of the rest of us, and we all went down in a chain reaction. Three girls were badly hurt. I had twelve stitches on my right knee. At the time it had been a heavily traveled road, but not one car crossed the bridge during the accident.

"When I got to the hospital I asked the doctor to put in an extra four stitches — I wanted to beat the Wandering Wheels record of fifteen! But he wouldn't do it. He said I didn't need them, and he couldn't find any place to put them.

"At first I think the guys were jealous that we girls had entered the Wandering Wheels program, because it had originally been set up with a masculine image. But I don't think they mind now."

Davenport describes Diane Lundquist as "a slender, queenly gal. Petite, womanly, attractive, poised, socially with it." Diane said she wanted to go along on a Wandering Wheels trip because it was "sort of a status thing on campus.

"Not that it should be that way, but I think that's the way it is. To be truthful, I was envious of the guys. Ever since my freshman year I had heard about the program. I never thought the girls would get a chance to go; so when we did, I grabbed it!

"The trip, I think, gave each of us a chance to look at ourselves. It brought the real you out in the difficult situations. I remember thinking, 'If I'm really going to be a Christian and show people what I've got as a Christian, I've got to be consistent.' I found living Christianity a lot easier than putting on a front.

"At first I was scared to tell people along the way what we were trying to accomplish on our trip, but soon I found I could easily express what I believed about God and His relationship to me.

"Even though the girls' trip was not supposed to be hard, it seemed to me that every time we came to a hill it was always *up* — we never coasted. One day I was so sore I could hardly get off my bike. We all laid down exhausted, and most of us were crying. The guys laid down too, and mocked us.

"I think our hardest day was the ride across the Everglades. It was seventy-five miles, and we had to make it in one day. It was the most boring ride — nothing to look at. Once, I think, I saw a bird, but little else except swamp, bugs, and a few Indian huts.

"But don't get me wrong; I'd do it again tomorrow, given the chance. I really miss the closeness of the kids. Every time we see each other, it's like we are brothers and sisters. We went through it together. I actually think I'm a happier person for having done it. And people have told me that my personality has changed because of it."

Since that first girls' tour, the coed trips have become a part of the Wandering Wheels program. A second coed trip was taken at Inter-term in 1970, and a third during the Easter recess that same year. Some of the girls have even been talking to Davenport about an all-girl cross-country trip in the near future.

Of course, girls never seem to be able to get enough sun, and according to Davenport, much of their motivation for riding on the coed trips is to get a suntan. "Either the girls expose themselves to the sun more than the fellas, or they're just not able to take as much sun at one time, but we've always had a couple of girls who get over-exposed," Davenport claims. "Their eyes will swell up and their hands will get puffy, making them far less attractive than if they had stayed out of the sun altogether. One gal got so much of her facial tissue swollen that it closed her eyes. We had to let her ride in the truck until she could see again.

"Girls are tigers, though. One gal, Margie, was reacting to the sun, too. But instead of riding in the truck, she wrapped herself in a scarf and put on a golf cap with a big bill; she looked like a bandit riding down the road."

On the January, 1970, coed trip, Davenport was leading a group between Miami and Tallahassee and encountered two days of rain. Finally, the sun broke out from behind the clouds just as the riders reached the Gulf coast. They all ran down to the beach to get all the sun they wanted.

A number of the riders went in swimming and to play around in the high breakers. Davenport waded in himself and was having a good time fighting the current when suddenly he noticed a girl near him with a frantic look on her face. "Are you all right?" he asked.

"No," she answered. "I need help."

She told Davenport that she couldn't make it back to shore, that the undertow was slowly taking her farther out. Davenport grabbed her by the hand and pulled her to shore where she dropped to the beach exhausted. Then he realized there were other girls in the same danger. He called to some of the fellows to help him, and together they pounded back into the surf.

"Some of the gals were to the place that they could barely touch bottom," Davenport recalls. "I swam out to another girl who was so scared she could hardly communicate."

He reached out to grab her and suddenly lost his footing. "Hey!" he yelled to one of the guys on an air mattress. "Help! We need help!" But the young man was too far away to reach them.

Davenport took a deep breath and sank to the bottom, touched, then pushed off with his feet and pushed the girl toward the shore. "I was just about at the razor's edge," he says. "Everyone else was busy helping the other girls. I never came closer to losing a life in the Wandering Wheels than right then. And I wasn't too sure whose life it would be. I was to the place where I was about to have to decide whether to save the girl or myself!"

Davenport continued to sink, touch, and push toward the shore. Finally, he had enough footing so he could walk around the girl and haul her in to the shore. Another swimmer was able to free himself to help him.

After the ordeal, three of the girls collapsed. Davenport started counting the kids and came up one short. He turned toward the sea and scanned the breakers. No one. He counted again. Still short. He sent one of the kids to check the johns. No one.

Several of the other Wheels began running around in a panic, trying to find the missing swimmer. Three minutes later the girl returned. She hadn't even been near the water. "When she showed up, we just sank to our knees on the beach and thanked God for His protection and deliverance. We nearly lost three girls that day," he says.

Near tragedies like these seem to knit a group together — or it's the frivolity at the other extreme. At a stop at Perry, Florida, on one of the coed trips, the entire group was crowded into a small council chambers for their night's rest.

If there is one thing that seems to drive the girls crazy, Davenport noticed, it was the guys' snoring. And the guys knew all about it. That night they had arrived late, and the riders knew they had some fifty miles of hills the next day, so they all settled down quickly.

Just about the time everyone had dozed off to sleep, one of the guys beat them to it and began snoring. Davenport could hear the girls whispering back and forth about "that vulgar sound."

The other guys caught on quickly and started faking their snores. It just about tore the girls apart. "Stop that!" they begged in loud whispers.

One girl became so disturbed that she crawled out of her sleeping bag, took her pillow, and headed across the darkened room toward the snoring rider. When she got there, she hit him with the pillow, and the pillow broke.

"It must have contained the world's lightest feathers," says Davenport. "Here we were in a pitch-black room, forty kids trying to sleep, and this pillow breaks. There were feathers everywhere. If you breathed too hard, you'd suck them into your mouth. The kids just about cracked up."

Davenport told everyone to go back to sleep. After the feathers had a night to settle, they could be cleaned up in the morning. The next morning the group spent several hours picking up the feathers by hand. "You couldn't sweep them," he says, "They'd just fly around again."

There have been similar situations when the guys would prank around and the girls would try to get back at them. One night the guys were irritating the girls; so the girls decided they would "attack" them with their pillows. Davenport could see their silhouettes and could tell what they were up to. So he waited for them all to make it out of their sleeping bags, stand up, and creep over to the fellows' side of the room. Just about the time they got there, Davenport slipped out of his sleeping bag and switched on the lights.

The girls stood there in their night clothes, their hair all done up in curlers. When the lights flashed on, they turned and went screaming back to their sleeping bags.

"It's been good to know that in a program that is dedicated wholly to God that these kids are able to live together in a mature spirit and have good, clean fun in a situation that some might think is traditionally taboo."

With the exception of the few who have a romantic interest in

166

". . . the girls can pretty well handle themselves."

each other before the coed trips, most of the girls and fellas look
out for each other as brothers and sisters would. The guys are
around to provide protection along the way, but the girls can pretty
well handle themselves. In a St. Petersburg, Florida, coffee house
one night, several of the riders mixed with the other young people
who were there, sharing with them some of their experiences on
their cycling trip and telling them how they were finding God
relevant to their lives.

One girl took an interest in one of the guys at a table, sat down, and began talking with him. He had the usual long hair hanging down to his shoulders, and a large earring in one ear.

Later, Davenport found that he had offered her some kind of drug, which she refused, explaining that she wasn't interested in taking drugs. When she told him she was "a Christian," that kind of turned him off. But then he asked her to go for a walk.

She consented, and as they were walking, he propositioned her. The girl took the invitation calmly, but again refused on the grounds that she was a Christian. He said he couldn't understand what difference that made.

She explained that as a Christian she wanted to follow the Christian teaching about sexual relationships, and as far as going to bed with a man, she was saving herself for the man God intended for her.

That did it! The guy left her in a huff.

The next day, however, he came back and asked forgiveness for the way he had acted. "I've never met a gal like you," he told her. "I'm glad you stood up for your standards. And I'm glad you were able to tell me why you feel the way you do."

Davenport thinks it was her Christian love, more than her Christian "ethic" that impressed the guy. Maybe the gals can't match the guys in the physical rigors of the Wandering Wheels program, but they have no difficulty in the spiritual realm, he says.

Perhaps the meaning of the Wandering Wheels program, whether the participants are girls or fellows, is best expressed in the proverb of a black Louisiana farmer the riders met during one of their trips. The conversation somehow had turned toward the discussion of religion, and the man said something that those who heard it have not forgotten. He said, "If a man say he likes cornbread, and he don't eat cornbread, then he is a liar."

The Wandering Wheels practice what they preach.

21

The apparent success of the cycling program in the sixties has encouraged the Wandering Wheels to expand its activities into the seventies. Hopefully, it will prove attractive to other segments of the world's youth. Incorporating the same principles of travel, excitement, tough physical discipline, and the pride of legitimate accomplishment, the Wandering Wheels plan to expand the program at home and overseas.

By the end of the 1968 tour, actually, after the program was five years old, Davenport knew that he had a good thing going just traveling with kids. He felt he could honestly hope to compete for their minds and bodies and, as he puts it, relate "Christ to them," if his program remained tough enough — if it was up-to-date and competitive with the misuse of drugs, sex, and the movies.

"So often the church has negated many areas of life without being positive," he says. "Here, we have a program that is right and good. We're fighting the bad by doing the good. We so often beat the drums on the no-no's without having the courage to create some alternatives. So far, God has given us confidence in a program that is attractive to kids.

"Kids want to move," he says. "They have a real craving to get away from that boob-tube and experience some of the things they have seen happening."

Desiring to continue to capitalize on this feeling, Davenport began to think about other ways to travel with kids. He remembered when he traveled with the UCLA football team around the United States. After each game he would always slip down on the floor of the plane to sleep. That recollection made him realize that it really wouldn't take much to make kids comfortable — just a thin mattress and the hum of wheels to lull them to sleep — and he could move the kids from spot to spot for cycling trips.

At the end of the summer of 1968 Davenport rented a camper shell and bolted it down to his red pickup, then took a two-by-four and bolted that along the back of the shell, put in some cots and had room to sleep three kids on top and three on the bottom. With three more in the truck cab, he had nine kids headed for the Atlantic.

He charged each kid a penny a mile for the overnight trip. The only time they stopped was to pick up more gas and to use the washrooms. Then they'd switch riders and the others would fall back asleep again. When everyone woke up in the morning they were on the East Coast. They rented surfboards and went surfing all day.

They did that twice in 1968. Davenport found that the ocean had a tremendous appeal to young people. And of equal interest to him: "The ocean was a great stage on which to present Jesus Christ. It was simple to talk about Christ after playing in the surf all day. You've proved yourself as an 'all-right-guy.' Kids are willing to listen to what you have to say."

In 1969 Davenport did the same thing with a white truck and a twelve-foot by eight-foot trailer bed. He put a camper on top of the trailer bed and rigged it up so it could sleep seventeen people. Again he put three others up front to share the driving, installed lights inside the camper so the riders could study or play cards, and took off for the ocean.

It took only fourteen hours to reach the ocean and cost the riders only twelve dollars each for the round trip, including the rental of surfboards and cost of meals.

In his office on the Taylor University campus, Davenport has a large map on which he has drawn a circle enclosing everything within a five-hundred-mile radius of the Upland, Indiana, campus. He knows he can reach any of those areas before morning: Kansas City, Minneapolis, Washington, D.C., Atlanta, Raleigh, Little

Rock, and the Smoky Mountain region. The Smoky Mountains have become a favorite.

"One thing we've learned," says Davenport. "You can't build a place like the Smokies for all the money in the world. You can build a Disneyland for several million dollars, but what a thrill to go and play at the real thing — lakes, streams, mountains. . . . "

Davenport is convinced that our highway systems (the Interstates) are "the greatest invention of modern man, truly a wonder of the world." Cruising at high speeds, Davenport can get nearly any place he wants in a short period of time — using a billion-dollar facility for very little cost.

"Our idea in the Wandering Wheels was *not* to build a building and bring in sounds and sights to display on a screen, but to get a piece of equipment that would move us out from our initial environment to a new one — overnight."

During the Thanksgiving school recess in 1969, Davenport asked a group of fellows and girls from a Goshen, Indiana, Methodist church on a four-day, five-night trip to Florida and back. They left Wednesday night before Thanksgiving Day, drove all night, played in the Smokies all day Thursday, ate Thanksgiving dinner, got back in the truck and drove all Thursday night, woke up at Daytona Beach, Florida, Friday morning, played all day Friday and Saturday at the beach, got back in the truck Saturday night, and headed back home. On the way back they stopped at the Methodist headquarters in Chattanooga, Tennessee, then climbed aboard again, and arrived back home Sunday night. It cost each kid only $28 — 2,800 miles at 10¢ a mile.

Davenport took twenty-one guys and gals on that trip, and they couldn't wait to get back to school to tell the kids what they did over the holiday weekend.

Davenport has used the truck in the winter time, too, to take kids skiing. He gets them out of school for one day; they leave Wednesday night, ski all day Thursday, drive back all night Thursday, and arrive in time for the kids to be back in classes on Friday — all rested.

For the Wandering Wheels, the truck and trailer concept has proved it has unlimited possibilities.

In 1970 the Lilly Endowment gave the Wandering Wheels organization some money with which to experiment. Davenport bought a bus, took out the seats, blacked out the windows, put in thirty beds, gave it a fancy paint job (pin stripes and all), carpeted the floor, installed a stereo unit donated by the Delco Remy Company in Kokomo, Indiana, for the kids to listen to, chromed the bumpers, and built a galley in the side. Each bed has a light over it, so the rider can study. Surfboards (or skis) can be carried on top. A few extra sleeping bags can be placed in the aisle, so the bus can carry thirty-five. Now he began moving out to many of the places within the five-hundred-mile radius of the Taylor campus.

Davenport calls it his "rolling bunkhouse concept" — trucking groups of young people to national recreation areas, to ballparks, to Broadway, to great rallies in the nation's capital.

In the near future he hopes to move fifty-thousand miles a year. On an eleven- or twelve-day run he estimates he can hit every major national park in America west of Indiana — the Grand Canyon, Yosemite, Yellowstone, Glacier — for a small amount of money. He figures that in one year alone he can touch fifteen hundred young people and spend sixty hours with each kid.

"You can't match what it will cost us with what it would cost a church to do the same thing," he says. "For this generation, being able to move about and letting kids hang loose will give more return on the dollar than anything else."

Davenport is also planning on developing a motorcycle program in the Wandering Wheels. Remember that he has found a high degree of interest in the "service" motorcycles he has used in his recent trips. "It is the single most attractive piece of equipment we have had, to bring the kids in hot pursuit," he says. "The motorcycle can be used efficiently and safely with kids."

Already on the "drawing boards" is a plan which calls for the use of six motorcycles on a trip from El Paso, Texas, to the Canadian border. Davenport would place two riders on each motorcycle, making room for twelve. They would move along the unpaved back roads of the nation for about fifteen days.

Davenport even envisions a motorcycle drill team which can perform on a non-professional basis at various public functions. If possible, he would like to introduce a similar idea for competition among colleges.

In 1971 the Wandering Wheels will be heading for Europe for a bicycle trip. All the other phases of the Wandering Wheels program are not to detract from the bicycle program. Davenport is also considering a cycling trip in Australia. And, way down the road, he hopes he may find some property out west, about ten miles off a highway, where kids can come and live apart from their usual pattern of living — a commune of about one thousand acres, where young people, if they want to, can come and live off the land and relate with their Creator.

Meantime, young people are still crowding to be a part of the Wandering Wheels cycling program. Some of the alumni have started cycling tours of their own. It has become a status thing with many of them. "You haven't lived until you've pedaled across the U.S. at least once," they say.

For Davenport the Wandering Wheels program has fulfilled his earlier vision to attract the attention of today's young people. It has met his concern that "the church have a program that kids would be willing to stand in line for."

As the Wandering Wheels cycle into the seventies, the young people seem to be doing just that — standing in line to become one of the Wandering Wheels.